MW00998580

KOKA

A Passion for Ikebana

48 Tales of Flowers and Branches

Koka Fukushima

Translated by Janine Beichman

First Edition
All translations in this book are by Janine
Beichman unless otherwise noted.
"Flower 1," from Makoto Ooka, *Ooka Makoto
Zen Shishu* (Tokyo: Shichosha, 2002), is
translated and reproduced with the kind
permission of Kaneko Ooka [Saki Fukase].
ISBN-978-4-600-00677-8
For inquiries please contact
book@kokanote.com

KOKA – 4

Flower 1

Makoto Ooka

Seeded in infinite softness,

with what majesty the flower stands

In its presence I cannot melt into air

I cannot even become a shadow

And I will never know

the scent-soaked embrace of the flower's fertilization

Through a space nested within waves of shining air

the flower races, more dashing than a ship in full sail…

I could not catch it

if I tried

Table of Contents
Preface

SPRING

SUMMER

Autumn

Winter

KOKA – 8

Preface

I was at a roundtable discussion with my friend the haiku poet Kai Hasegawa when he turned to me and asked, "What is the difference between *ikebana* and [Western] flower arrangement?"

"In flower arrangement, you use flowers to fill in a space. In *ikebana*, you use flowers and branches to make a space come alive," I retorted almost without thinking. My remark was rooted in a feeling about *ikebana* that, without my being clearly aware of it, has taken shape in me over the years of my practice in Japan and around the world. Kai later expanded on it in *The Idea of Wa*. His exposition was made with such skill that that part of his book is now used in high school and college entrance exams.

Kai also invited me to write about plants for Café Kigosai, a haiku website that he began. Eight years on, I am still writing for it. I put together the first forty-eight pieces and published them as a book called *Hana no Terasu de*. Then I decided to publish an English version and asked Janine Beichman to translate it. This is the book you are now reading.

It was through the poet Makoto Ooka, who is the author of "Flower 1," the epigraph to this book, and his wife, Kaneko Ooka [Saki Fukase], that I came to know both Kai and Janine. I am very grateful for the good luck that led me to them.

The forty-eight tales you are about to read tell of my encounters with the various plants I have met in the near-half century of my life and work in *ikebana*. I hope with all my heart that they bring you much pleasure. 🌱

Spring

SPRING

1 Forsythia

Forsythia suspensa
連翹 *rengyo*

Bright yellow flowers herald the coming of spring.

One bitterly cold day in early January, I was strolling through a wholesale flower market in Helsinki when some forsythia in a bucket caught my eye. I knew it could not have been grown in Finland, of course, where even the bays were still frozen over. Nor was it likely to have come with the many other flowers imported from the Netherlands, for even there it was still not warm enough for forsythia to bloom. No, surely the blaze of yellow must have come from somewhere farther south. What a long journey it must have made to bring tidings of spring!

At year's end, we have wintersweet, and then Japanese cornel for the New Year. Come spring, the yellow forsythia and Japanese witch hazel flowers, which bloom even before their tiny new leaves appear, shimmer with vitality.

The branches of the forsythia often have delicate, flowing curves, but since they are hollow, they resist being shaped into curved lines. They are one of the so-called "unbendable and easy to break" (*tame ga kikanai*) flowering materials that we use as is in *ikebana*.

As spring warms the soil, you find forsythia, still leafless, growing wild in country lanes, on hillsides, and in fields. By early summer, most of the beautiful flowering branches of the spring have disappeared from the flower shops. Then the forsythia, with its beautiful green foliage, begins to appear in our flower arrangements instead.

Forsythia originated in China but can now be found in many parts of the world. Some years ago, at the residence of the Japanese

Forsythia

ambassador in Seoul, I came upon a vivid yellow border of forsythias lining a long, narrow path to the embassy residence. Sometimes I think of it now and wonder if that gorgeous yellow is still there.

When I am abroad, I usually find very few branches of any kind at the local florists'. Once, for a workshop I gave in Abu Dhabi, I assumed that if any were to be had, the selection would be limited and in rather poor condition. I was surprised to be told that there would be no problem in obtaining forsythia branches for our demon-stration. The many UAE ladies who attended, all clothed in black abayas, laughed and chatted as they arranged the forsythia branches. The small yellow flowers seemed to dance among the black of their cloaks. The heat, so much more intense there than it ever gets in Japan, lent the yellow a special verve.

Peaceful scenes show forsythia off at its best. 🌿

Forsythia

2 Japanese Witch Hazel

Hamamelis japonica

万作 *mansaku*

Many years ago, Morishige Hisaya, the wonderful actor who later played Tevye in the Japanese version of *Fiddler on the Roof*, starred in a television drama called *Witch Hazel Flowers*. I was a child then, so most of the drama went right over my head, although I do remember wondering what the title had to do with witch hazel flowers.

I never did figure out the connection, but at least now I know, thanks to my botanical dictionary, the possible origins of the flower's name. *Mansaku*, as Japanese witch hazel is called, may come from *mazu-saku*, "to bloom first," because the unusually shaped yellow flowers appear before the leaves. The tangle of thread-like petals almost suggests some unique Asian sweet.

Another possible derivation of the Japanese name points to *mansaku* as a shortened form of *honen mansaku*, "a year of abundance." Spring flowers, including those of the witch hazel, were thought to predict a good autumn harvest since they appear in such abundance so early in spring. Their size, their color, and the fullness of their blooms were often associated with autumn's fruits.

Japan, North America, and China all have native varieties of witch hazel which have been selectively bred in Japan and the West into many kinds of ornamentals, including the safflower red *akabana mansaku*, "red-flowered witch hazel." Japanese and North American witch hazel have different botanical names (*Hamamelis japonica* and *Hamamelia virginiana*, respectively) but look almost alike.

In English, the "hazel" of witch hazel might suggest the hazelnut, but, in fact, it refers here to the hazelnut tree, a member of the birch

Japanese Witch Hazel

family. "Witch" was originally spelled "wiche," or "wyche," and meant "pliant, supple," as the branches of this plant notably are. But this old meaning fell away along with its spelling, and "witch" to modern ears means "sorceress." Such creatures have a problematic image, to say the least, but when I look at witch hazel flowers I often imagine mischievous little witches merrily running up and down the branches.

In *ikebana*, we use witch hazel in every season except winter. After the yellow flowers fade, the leaves, as beautiful in their own way as the flowers, appear. In autumn, the round, green leaves of late spring and summer turn to red, orange, and orange-yellow. At each season, the branches, whether laden with flowers or leaves, are easy to coax into attractive shapes for our arrangements. 🌱

Japanese Witch Hazel

3 Camellia

Camellia japonica

椿 *tsubaki*

Over two thousand garden varieties of camellia have been bred from the wild camellia native to Japan. There are camellia aficionados in every corner of the world who can identify a variety by the leaves alone and even describe the flowers before they bloom.

The Japanese character for "camellia" (*tsubaki*) is itself made up of two characters (see above right). The character *ki*, on the left, means "tree," while the character on the right, *haru*, means "spring." While the camellia can be used in *ikebana* even in the wintertime, I like it best from early spring until its season of full bloom.

The camellia embodies the three principles on which *ikebana* is based: line, color, and mass, thus offering the *ikebana* practitioner opportunities for a broad range of expression. As the season comes into full swing, and different varieties of camellia bloom in more and more colors and shapes, I find it hard to resist the temptation to arrange their beauty.

I belong to the Sogetsu School of Ikebana, which teaches *ikebana* in Japan and in many other countries around the world. About seventeen years ago, when a new *iemoto* (head) of our school of *ikebana* assumed the leadership role, the bilingual English-Japanese textbook we use underwent revision. During the process, we drew up a table of contents and asked our overseas branches for feedback before drafting the textbook itself and preparing the illustrations. In response, we got some comments that made me think that the Japanese concept of a flower might be rather special, in the sense that it firmly includes branches and leaves as well as blossoms.

Camellia

For example, in reference to the curriculum section "With Flowers Only," we were surprised to be asked whether we cut the stalk of the flower off before arranging it. I realized then that our readers abroad might have a perception of the camellia that is different from that of the Japanese.

It was in New Zealand or Australia that I saw a tree with so many camellias in bloom that the branches were all but invisible. I wondered if it was purposely pruned to grow like that, or if it had been bred that way because the flowers were preferred to foliage.

In Japan, you sometimes see fallen camellias on the ground. If you look up at the tree from which they dropped, the branches are spread out wide above you and may even be swaying in the breeze. In the smaller Shinto shrines and other locations where the plants are left to grow pretty much on their own, I have found camellia trees whose thickly clustered leaves create their own twilit space even during the daytime. For us, the leaves and branches are every bit as attractive as the flowers.

When it comes to the Japanese camellia, as we use it in *ikebana*, we can stress the subtle flow of a branch's curve, or we can mass a quantity of the deep green leaves to create a sense of vitality. We can also use a single flower figuratively, to express a feeling, or to suggest an abstract thought. The Japanese camellia allows us to do any and all of these things. It contains within itself the seeds of many stories.

Now that spring is here again, I pick one up, imagining an arrangement that might convey at least a hint of these myriad possibilities. ❦

Camellia

4 Flowering Peach

Prunus persica

花桃 *hana-momo*

Towns and villages famous for their peach blossoms see most of their visitors after the Peach Blossom Festival (also called the Doll Festival or Girls' Day) has ended. This ancient festival was originally celebrated on the third day of the third month of the lunar calendar, when the blossoms were in bloom, but is now celebrated according to the solar calendar, on March 3, which is earlier. Peach flowers are traditionally arranged on that day.

Getting perfect blossoms to market in time for the Peach Blossom Festival is a feat. The cut branches are stored in hothouses where the temperature is controlled to provide appropriate climate conditions regardless of the weather outside. The moist, warm air promotes not only the early appearance of blossoms but also of leaves, which are not desirable in the arrangements we do for this festival. In order to prevent the emergence of leaves, growers cut the peach branches early.

When the flower buds have reached the desired size, they are wrapped in bunches in black plastic sheets to shut out the sunlight, which arrests further development. Then the growers deliver the branches to the flower market and to the flower shops. The buds may still be stiff, but the flowers will bloom in no time when they are brought into a warm environment. The flowering peach, native to China, was known in Japan from the Nara period, when it brightened many gardens. Those early trees may have resembled the one the renowned poet Ootomo Yakamochi described in a poem from the eighth-century *Man'yoshu* (*The Collection of Ten Thousand*

Flowering Peach

Leaves), the earliest collection of poetry in Japanese:

> In a spring garden
> the deep pink glow of
> peach blossoms
> lights up the path below,
> and there she's come to linger—
> a young girl

> *Haru no sono/kurenai niou/momo no hana/*
> *shitaderu michi ni/idetatsu otome*

There are many varieties of flowering peach. The multilayered type is used for the Peach Blossom Festival. Then there is the single-layered type, the chrysanthemum peach (*Amygdalus persica* cv. Stellata), which resembles its namesake, and several kinds of "weeping" varieties. The color may be white or pink—or even both colors on the same branch, as in the Genpei peach blossom.

When the flowering peach is featured as the principal flower material in an *ikebana* class, a student will sometimes say, "I'm going to take the peach blossoms home. If I unwrap them here, the flowers will fall off and the branches will be bare." It's true. Peach branches come tied together with string, which you must carefully snip from top to bottom, while holding the tips of the branches together. Some people go from bottom to top, which is fine too. The important thing is to cut very carefully and spread the bundled branches out as you go. Coaxing the straight branches into shapes is not impossible, but the flowers do tend to scatter when you do so. We prefer to use them as they are.

In the auditorium that we use for *ikebana* demonstrations, the audience can enjoy watching the process as an arrangement takes shape before their very eyes. On one occasion the demonstrator was a very experienced teacher who created several beautiful works one after the other. When the time came for the very last one, a cry of surprise arose from observers as several branches of flowering peach in full bloom, the largest ones nearly three meters high (about ten feet), were carried onto the stage, swaying back and forth. One after the other, the teacher placed them in several vases, each the height of a person. Then she began to cut and trim, as several assistants raced about picking up branches as they fell. Each time the teacher took hold of a branch, fully open blossoms shook loose and fluttered to the floor. With each step she took, the petals that had scattered at her feet danced up in the air.

As I watched this scene, I realized why the wooden floor of the stage had been completely covered with a black carpet that day.

Then it was over, and the assistants instantly vanished. The carpet lay blanketed in petals. From above some were still drifting down. The demonstrator stood beneath them, a radiant smile on her round face as she bade farewell to the audience and thanked them for coming. "Today," she said, "it was my pleasure to show you Peach Blossoms in Spring, the earthly paradise of Shangri-La."

She has been gone for quite a few years, but I always think of her at this season.

We have fallen camellias and swirling cherry blossoms—and then these flowering peach blossoms, whose scattering is so beautiful. There are so many kinds of beauty waiting to be discovered among flowers. When the flower arranger discovers new beauty in a flower she knows well, she experiences a moment of pure bliss. 🌸

Flowering Peach

5
Oriental Paperbush

Edgeworthia chrysantha

三椏 *mitsumata*

I first held Oriental paperbush in my hand a long time ago at the beginning of my studies of *ikebana*. It was bleached, not fresh, and about eighty centimeters long (about two and a half feet). The pure white color was the result of its having been dried, peeled, and then chemically treated and bleached. I was told that unlike other plants it did not wilt in the summer heat and required no water, so you could design freely with it, and even beginners could enjoy arranging it.

The name in Japanese means "triple-branching," or "three again," depending on which kanji it is written with. Both versions make reference to the fact that the stems always branch off into three shoots. Paperbush is best known for its bark, which is the raw material for traditional *washi* paper and, sometimes (though not now so much as formerly), banknotes.

These days, besides seeing it in the wild, you sometimes see the fresh plants at flower markets, albeit for a brief time only, as materials for *ikebana*, with the flowering branches available until early spring. The stems are quite flexible, so you can bend them into almost any shape. When cut with scissors, a slightly sweet scent emanates from the exposed part.

Once, while strolling through a park in the center of the city, I came across a paperbush plant that was two meters tall (about six and a half feet). For paperbush, this is on the high side. Like the winter daphne, which blooms at around the same time, paperbush belongs to the Thymelaeaceae family. Its branches grow in graceful curves.

When it blooms, not a single leaf appears on the cinnamon-col-

Oriental Paperbush

ored branches. A close look reveals small, tubular flowers that look like clumps of very short, white, velvety hair, split at the tips and yellow or orange within. Gathered together, they form a single massed flower in the shape of a hemisphere. There seemed to be a hundred or more of these bunches of flowers on the paperbush I was looking at. The branches spread out in all directions, and the flowers seemed to be facing slightly downwards. The deep greens of the neighboring evergreens and the grays and browns of leafless boughs enhanced the vivid oranges and yellows of the flowers all the more.

With respect to bleaching, I am often asked what the process is that makes paperbush so white. (I am sometimes also asked, when I'm abroad, if the bleached Chinese fan palm, which is originally green, is made of paper!) I explain that even florists are not aware of how the bleaching process is carried out. When asked, they will say there's an unpleasant smell associated with it so it's done somewhere in the mountains—and thus remains a trade secret.

This plant with its tripartite branches has its little mysteries. 🌿

Oriental Paperbush

6 Violet

This pretty little purple flower does not often make an appearance in *ikebana* arrangements, perhaps because it is so short. But whenever I happen to see a bunch bound up tightly in a small container in a

Violet

flower shop, I cannot resist buying it.

Beloved around the world since ancient days, the violet has appeared in too many poems and songs to count. In Japan, it is even included in the poems of the eighth century *Man'yoshu*. We are told the violet originated in temperate regions. Where and how was it carried around the world, so that today it exists in virtually every corner of the globe and is said to have over 400 varieties? Of these, the one we see most often growing wild in Japan is the Manchurian violet.

One of my favorite songs is the elegant and uplifting "Violets for Your Furs." The lyrics are by Tom Adair and the music by Matt Dennis, and many artists have covered it, including Billie Holiday and Frank Sinatra. The song tells a story of lovers in Manhattan. Snow is falling everywhere, and the streets are icy, but when the man buys a bunch of violets for his lady love to pin on her fur coat, December seems like April. The violets work their magic, and the couple falls head over heels in love.

Several varieties of violet are native to North America, and I do not know which of those features in the song, but the flower could only be a violet, perhaps a hothouse one. Even the pansy, although bred from the violet, would never evoke the same mood. Living in the times we do, I like to sing this song about violets, with its warm romance and high style, during this cold season. 🌿

7 Aromatic Litsea

Litsea citriodora

青文字 *aomoji*

Come spring, someone handling aromatic litsea for the first time might well exclaim, "What a lot of fruit to bear at this time of year!" In fact, they would be talking about flower buds, not fruit. Small and round as they cling to the green branch, they certainly look like berries.

Lindera umbellata, or lindera, is another plant belonging to the laurel family. Called *kuromoji* in Japanese (in contrast to aromatic litsea, which is called *aomoji*), its branches, like those of aromatic litsea, are green, but they are speckled with black. Strips of the branches, bark and all, are often formed into hand-crafted tooth-picks and utensils for traditional sweets. Aromatic litsea of course can be used like that too, as you quickly realize when you cut off a small piece of the branch.

Try crushing one of the aromatic litsea's light green, round buds between your fingers and inhale deeply the restorative, citrusy aroma it gives off. Regardless of your state of mind, its lemony redolence never fails to soothe. It is easy to understand why aromatic litsea is used as a fragrance.

Before long, the buds unfold and come into their own as lively, pale yellow flowers with a greenish tint. Gradually these flowers turn white, and small as they are, there is something spirited and proud in the way they bloom. The tree itself can grow as high as seven meters (about twenty-three feet). Aromatic litsea is dioecious, so if you want to know what its autumn fruits look like, by all means buy and cultivate one male and one female plant.

Many plants of the laurel family are aromatic, but, although both aromatic litsea and lindera belong to the laurel family, the former is classified under the litsea genus and the latter under the lindera genus. 🌿

Aromatic Litsea   *Aromatic Litsea*

8 Flowering Cherry Tree

Prunus

桜 *sakura*

It must have been twenty years ago or so that I went to Saudi Arabia under the aegis of The Japan Foundation. Since the custom there is that men and women do not sit together in public, they asked that both teacher and assistant be female. Naturally, I complied.

Three nights before my departure I received an unexpected telephone call from the wife of the Japanese ambassador to Saudi Arabia who was then in Riyadh. She told me that flowers were delivered by plane from Europe twice a week, but in the last week there had been almost none that I would likely find suitable. "We really want to do a proper demonstration for the royal family," she said. "Could you possibly bring some flowers with you? I'll talk to the quarantine officials."

In our school of *ikebana*, we try to use plants native to wherever we are holding our demonstration. Especially when overseas, we like to use materials that participants are familiar with so that they feel closer to *ikebana*. Normally, we begin with the local flower markets, and, if we need more, we ask permission to get plants from private and botanical gardens. In a desert climate like Saudi Arabia's, and in the limited time we had to prepare, this approach did not look promising.

My route from Japan called for spending one night in Paris and flying early the following morning to Riyadh. I knew that if I were to bring materials from Japan, I would need to leave them at the airport in Paris overnight. I was extremely worried that the flowers would not stay fresh.

Flowering Cherry Tree

For the demonstration at the ambassador's residence, ladies wrapped in abayas arrived one after another in their luxury cars. Since abayas all look identical, each was placed in a plastic bag with a name and number and laid on a table when the ladies checked them at the cloakroom. With the removal of the black abayas, the demonstration hall shone with elegant designer suits and dresses. The women-only hall looked more like a field of flowers in full bloom than part of a country strictly governed by religious rules.

The one meter long (three foot) blossoming cherry branches I had brought from Japan survived the trip and were almost in full bloom. When I walked on stage with an armful of them, a murmur of excitement spread through the audience. Questions came from every direction: "Are these flowers from Japan?" "How long will they last?" "What are they called?"

Both demonstrations, one for women only and one for men and women in the foreign diplomatic corps, went smoothly. After they were over, the ambassador's wife explained that she would be paying a sick call and said, "Someone very close to the king is in hospital, and I think she would really like to see some of the flowering cherry. Would you let me take some?"

The story doesn't end there. Rather a long time after we returned to Japan, when the ambassador and his wife were nearing the end of their tenure in Saudi Arabia, I received another phone call from the wife. She told me that the ambassador had been summoned by the king, who, her husband later informed her, said, "According to the interpreter, your efforts made a great contribution." Since Arabic has a singular "you" and a plural "you," and the king used the plural, she went on excitedly, "I felt he was including me in his thanks and immediately recalled the cherry blossoms from that occasion."

I looked back and remembered. When I received that first phone call from Saudia Arabia suggesting I bring flowers from Japan for the demonstration, I immediately phoned a florist from whom I had been ordering for many years. "Anything at all is fine," I began, "as long as it's not found in Saudi Arabia." But then, in a sudden burst of inspiration, I exclaimed, "Of course, the flowering cherry tree!" Perhaps the idea of flowering cherry came to me because it was spring and the boughs had begun to appear in the shops. "You're going to check them overnight at the airport in Paris?" said the florist. "You're taking a real chance. I hope the buds open in time."

Unbeknownst to me, the worried man shaved the bark off the end of each cut branch and placed it in a water-filled holder. Then he used wire to suspend the holders in the box so that the flowers would not touch each other. When I arrived at my destination and opened the box, I was filled with admiration for his superb craftsmanship.

Benefitting from the warm concern of everyone involved, the flowering cherry fulfilled its mission perfectly.

Flowering Cherry Tree

9
Japanese Wild Allspice

Lindera praecox

油瀝青 *aburachan*

When I teach *ikebana* in English, the English names for the plants we use always present problems. Even within the same country, the names of plants and flowers may differ from region to region.

Sometimes the Japanese name or the local one is easier to remember than one of the myriad English names a plant may have. At times, our discussions on the topic of naming have become so lively that they have left a deep impression on me.

I'll give you an example. The other day I was demonstrating an arrangement in class when one of my assistants came up to me and said several of the students were whispering amongst themselves about the fact that I had used the affectionate diminutive suffix *-chan*, which is reserved for use in families, for young children, and among longtime friends, to talk about a plant. I went up to the lectern and stated emphatically that I would never talk about a flower in that way. "The name of this material itself," I declared, "is *aburachan*."

Another name for the plant is *zusa*, which is what I was taught to call it the first time I arranged it. Like aromatic litsea and spicebush, it belongs to the laurel family. A subtle fragrance emanates from it when you cut it. The branches are quite flexible, which makes it easy to create shapes with them. Their small, pale yellow-green flowers spread outward to fill in the spaces.

As for the name of this plant, *abura*, which means "oil," refers to the oil secreted from the fruit, which at one time was used for lamps. According to the dictionary, *chan* is the residue left after distilling tar into (a different kind of) oil. Whoever first discovered this distillation process is worthy of great respect. The same goes for who-ever thought to combine the two words as the name for this tree.

My students who giggled at the name, and even someone like me who, to my shame, finds it hard to remember the names of flowers, can remember the name *aburachan* with no trouble. With its witty name, this plant must have provided moments of pleasure and relax-ation to many over the centuries.

It is a dioecious plant, and the male flowers are said to be larger than the female. Because of its fragrance, the English name is Japanese wild allspice. In this case, though, I would vote in favor of the Japanese name, *aburachan*. 🌿

Japanese Wild Allspice

10 Full Moon Maple

Acer japonicum

板屋楓 *itayakaede*

One of the varieties of maple we use in *ikebana* is the *itaya-kaede*, so called because the layering of its leaves resembles the overlapping configuration of the traditional wooden Japanese *itaya* ("folded-plate") roof.

When urban dwellers like myself want to use the branches of this kind of maple in our arrangements for exhibitions, we have to special-order it; city florists don't keep it in stock, because it is too difficult to keep fresh after being cut.

Sometimes it comes from the florist as an entire tree, with the root wrapped protectively in cloth. When that happens, I cut off branches directly from the tree but try to leave a few if possible. I like to leave the trunk, the main branch, and a few side branches too. Then I return it to the earth, roots and all, hoping that one day the branches will grow back and I can use it again.

Once the poet Makoto Ooka, whom I knew for many years, was to be interviewed for a television program at his home. His wife, Kaneko [Saki Fukase], to whom I was also close, called one day to ask if I could prepare a flower arrangement for the taping of the interview, which was to be in May. I ran over to their place with my *ikebana* tools to see what would be appropriate and decided that the one plant I wanted to use more than anything was the *itaya* maple. I stressed that in my order to the florist. On the day of the filming, a maple in full leaf and a bit shorter than I am was delivered, complete with roots, to the Ookas' home, and I arranged it in a rather large Bizen vase that they owned.

Full Moon Maple

When I watched the interview on the monitor, I could not help feeling pleased with my choice, for the fresh greenery made a lovely backdrop for the poet's gentle expression.

Later they planted the tree in the garden behind their house. In the autumn Kaneko called me and said, "Koka, your maple has the most beautiful foliage now." How happy I was that the maple had felt comfortable enough in their garden to put down permanent roots and show off its gorgeous leaves!

In *ikebana*, we lump several different kinds of large-leafed maples together under the name *itaya*. They all have especially bright and beautiful leaves. The branches wither quickly when exposed to air, so we place them in water before cutting them to the desired length. Then we shave the bark off with scissor blades and dip them in an unsweetened liquor like brandy or whisky for about ten seconds. At that point, they are ready to be arranged.

The green leaves open crisp and wide to welcome early summer and put us in a cheerful frame of mind. The seeds are shaped like tiny, two-winged propellers. The wind blows them far off and eventually they settle down and sprout in a new home.

Full Moon Maple

11 Carnation

Dianthus caryophyllus
カーネーション *kaneshon*

It goes without saying that a bouquet of flowers, especially carnations, is the signature gift for Mother's Day. The custom originated, according to American lore, near the beginning of the twentieth century, with a woman who handed out white carnations to friends at a gathering in memory of her deceased mother. Nowadays, carnations come not only in the classic red and white but also, thanks to biotechnology, in a variety of shapes and colors, including dark violet.

Once, when I gave a demonstration in Mexico, the mayor of the city where it was held hosted a banquet in my honor. Three days before, my assistant and I arrived in Mexico City, and the very next day I was scheduled to appear on television. As soon as the program was over, I checked to make sure that the flower containers and tools borrowed from the Mexico branch of the Sogetsu School of Ikebana, as well as our suitcases, were safely loaded into the car they had waiting for us. Then off we went on a drive of several hours to the city where the next demonstration was to be held.

What with the tight schedule and my jet lag, by the evening of the third day I was exhausted. It was sometime after sunset when we arrived at the mayor's official residence. Making our way along a path of lights at foot level, we found ourselves at the main entrance, where we were saluted by white-gloved military officers wearing uniforms decorated with red braid. I felt a twinge of apprehension and was very glad that I had packed a kimono (which I do not usually take with me when I go abroad) for the banquet.

The first thing to meet my eyes when I entered the huge dining

Carnation

room was a large Japanese flag hanging on the wall. It was about four feet wide. Up close I could see that it was woven out of white and red carnations. When I sat down and had a chance to look around, I could see that among the eighty (so I was told) Mexican guests, many were of Japanese descent.

After dinner, several of the Japanese Mexicans approached me. They wanted to thank me for coming to their corner of the world. They told me that they had been growing flowers there for a long time, but this was the first time they had been invited to dinner at the mayor's residence. "We are very grateful to you for this memorable day," they said.

I did not know how to reply, for it was not I who deserved their thanks, but our companion from The Japan Foundation. She had insisted on including this city in our itinerary, for she wanted to show *ikebana* not only to people who lived in the capital but to those in outlying areas as well.

The Japanese Mexicans who thanked me had grown the flowers for that flag on their own land, and I am certain that at the mayor's banquet, which was so important to them, they kept a close eye on the flag up to the last minute, to make sure all went well. It was I who owed them gratitude and thanks.

For this special day they had chosen the very best of their carnations and put all their heart into weaving them into a Japanese flag. There was no mistaking the attachment they felt to their Japanese roots. An intense desire to make Japan worthy of that attachment filled me.

12 Ornamental Onion

Allium

アリウム *ariumu*

Flower containers from the valuable collection of the Sogetsu Foundation had been lent to participants for one of our special exhibitions. On the day of preparation, as we were creating our arrangements, I noticed that my neighbor, who was using a white glass container by a famous artist, looked a little unhappy about something. Next to her, ten or so giant onions sat in a bucket, their round purple heads protruding from the wrapping paper.

When cut, this flower exudes an orange-colored sap from its stalk, so several days before, in order to release the sap, she had cut the stalks and placed them in water. But at the exhibition space, as soon as the scissors pierced them, the orange sap oozed out again and gradually dyed the water.

This is what we call the "bitterness" of the allium; if it stains your clothes, it is difficult to remove it. But my neighbor was more concerned in this case about the borrowed white glass container, whose interior surface was full of indentations in which a stain could hide forever.

Every morning for the period of the exhibition, she completely changed the water in the container, although I was unable to tell if she really succeeded in removing all the "bitterness."

The ornamental onion is distinguished by the way the small blossoms at the top of its stalk open outwards in an almost perfect sphere. The giant onion is especially interesting because its many small blossoms grow in a tangle atop the straight stalk, but, when you hold the stalk between your hands and twirl it about, the tangles come

Ornamental Onion

undone, and a pretty, round globe takes shape.

The smallish ball-head onion has a head which is reddish-purple on top and green below. It really does look a little like the head of the red-crowned crane, from which it takes its Japanese name, "red-crowned onion."

The ornamental leek has an odor which reminds you that ornamental onions belong to the same family as scallions. In fact, if you soak any sort of ornamental onion in water for a long time, the water takes on a scallion-like odor.

Both the ball-head onion and the ornamental leek have curved and twisted stems because they are purposely cultivated that way.

You sometimes see Schubert's allium (also called Schubert's onion) with a head almost sixteen inches in diameter. We, the members and students of the Sogetsu School, call it a "firecracker" among ourselves because it makes us think of an enlarged sparkler. It can be enjoyed in its natural state, but you can also dry it or color it and arrange it without water.

The stem of the giant onion is almost completely straight and has a big, globe-shaped head on which myriads of small purple flowers are neatly arrayed. When I see the contrast between the straight stem and the big round flower, I realize mother nature is a true artist.

Ornamental Onion

13 Delphinium

Delphinium
デルフィニウム *derufiniumu*

Cut flowers are said to last longer if you cut the stalks in water, although these days hardy varieties are cultivated which do not need such careful tending. It was not always so. Over the years, techniques had to be developed by *ikebana* practitioners to extend the life of flowers used in arrangements.

For example, delphinium has a large and hollow stalk of about one to one and a half meters (about five feet) in length. You hold it firmly upside down and, from a narrow-spouted pitcher, pour water straight down into the stalk. Then you pack it with paper as a kind of stopper and return it to the water. It seems this is no longer the practice, but I think it was a good strategy.

Delphinium is one of the many varieties of ornamental larkspur, and it comes in a number of colors—sky-blue, white, deep purple, lavender. These days one even sees yellow, pink, and something close to red.

Delphinium is both the botanical and the common name for this flower. It is said to come from "delphis," the Greek word for "dolphin," probably because among the many varieties of this flower there was one which resembled a dolphin.

Delphinium is also known as "flying swallow grass" in Japanese (so the story goes) because when the petals lengthen and become spurs the flowers resemble swallows in flight. (Spurs refer to the hollow extension of the petals and calyx.) The shape suggests a comparison to birds (larks and swallows) and mammals (dolphins).

Even if you arrange only one tall spike of delphinium in a con-

Delphinium

tainer, its elegance and stature extend beyond the arrangement and give the entire space around it an expansive feeling. You must take care, however, because, due to its height and the hollow stalk, the delphinium breaks easily. In order to stabilize it, a thick wire is sometimes carefully drawn through the stalk.

The flowers start blooming from the bottom up, but if you cut them away as they wither, quite a few pretty ones remain. Even a single flower can be used in a number of ways.

In Portugal I was once invited to lunch at the home of a Japanese lady who lived in Lisbon. In the middle of the table was a black-lacquered board on which about ten blue delphinium flowers of various sizes were scattered about, together with some white roses. Handsomely threading them together was a length of green ivy freshly picked from the garden.

Line, color, mass—the three important elements required for *ikebana*—were all there. With the flowers so perfectly laid out and set off against the black backdrop, the flat surface of the lacquered board acquired a new dimension. This method of displaying flowers by spreading them out is called *shikibana* and is another expression of *ikebana*.

One might leave a finished arrangement in a container as is for several days, then remove the well-watered flowers, leaving them free to express a different aspect of themselves when reused in other arrangements, such as having them lie directly on a lacquered board. This kind of expression is possible not only with larkspur, but with any kind of flower that can do without water for a limited time.

I was in Portugal to give *ikebana* demonstrations that time, and this was my first Japanese meal in a while. Thanks to the thoughtfulness of my hostess, so knowledgeable and wise about flowers, I spent a blissful afternoon in Lisbon and felt totally revived. 🌸

14 Baby's Breath

Gypsophila

霞草 *kasumiso*

When I am overseas, gathering materials for an *ikebana* demonstration generally begins with a visit to a wholesale flower market. As I mentioned earlier, in "Flowering Cherry" (Chapter 8), it also sometimes involves visits to private as well as botanical gardens.

The suburbs of Quito, Ecuador, where I once went for a demonstration, are famous for their flower growers. Even before I visited the wholesale market in town, I asked the Japanese embassy staff there to take me to a flower farm. As soon as I entered the hut where cut flowers were kept, I saw a bucket crammed full of clumps of fluffy white baby's breath. I had never seen so much at once. "Please take as many bucketsful as you like," the owner of the farm said, and I happily complied, all the while wondering how much such a quantity would cost in Japan. What a treat it was!

My assistant and I gathered up the baby's breath and took it to the event site, where we tried to make it look even fluffier and more buoyant by stripping off all the small leaves and trimming the already bent and broken branches, which snap so easily even in their natural state. Before that, we had removed the roots of all the plants, along, of course, with the soil attached to them, which was the more difficult chore.

"That's enough baby's breath for some time," I exclaimed suddenly as I looked down at my hands, blackened with dust and the sap-like substance that oozed from the plants.

On another trip, to Los Angeles, I saw a variety of baby's breath at the wholesale flower market that had been carefully cultivated

Baby's Breath

and was wonderfully tall. There was not as much of it as there had been in Quito, but I bought quite a lot and used it on stage for the finale of the demonstration I did there.

The instant they brought the baby's breath to me onstage, and I was about to arrange it, I sneezed. My nose tingled, and my eyes felt itchy. I was unsure what it was, whether it was the distinctive smell of baby's breath or whether they had applied too much pesticide. Luckily, I was able to get someone who was due to arrive from Tokyo the next day to bring me some medicine. My symptoms continued for several days after the demonstration.

Baby's breath comes in both pink and white, single- and double-layered varieties. It can be dried (both varieties) or colored (the double-layered variety) for use in *ikebana*. In the latter case, the stem is soaked in colored water. It tends to play a supporting role in arrangements. Its softly enveloping gentleness goes well with its Japanese name, *kasumiso* (mist flower). But don't be fooled. Haven't we all known a graceful and loving beauty whose image dims the more we get to know her? 🌱

15

Yesterday-Today-and-Tomorrow

Brunfelsia latifolia
勾蕃茉莉 *nioibanmatsuri*

In mid-April, the branches of the yesterday-today-and-tomorrow that I keep in a flower pot on my veranda burst forth with new purple buds. I have never seen cut flowers from this plant in a flower shop, but in early summer you can sometimes buy them in pots. The flower has five overlapping petals which start out as purple, with just a bit of white at the center, like an eye. Gradually, the purple fades to lavender and then white, so that the shrub has blooms in all three colors simultaneously, creating a very lively effect.

There are other plants that flower in different colors simultaneously, like honeysuckle, which varies from white to yellow, and the cotton rosemallow (*Hibiscus mutabilis* cv. Versicolor), which varies from pale white to pink and, in the evening, darker pink, but I cannot think of any others which change from a deep purple to white.

In Japanese, the name of this flower includes characters which mean "scent" and "foreign." In fact, their scent is so strong at their peak (a little like jasmine) that if I walk out onto the terrace at night, I can tell they are in full bloom even in the dark. It is thought that the flower was imported to Japan from its native South America in the early twentieth century.

The English name "yesterday-today-and-tomorrow" is very apt for this plant whose color changes so quickly. The name reminds me of an Italian anthology film of the same name (*Ieri Oggi Domani*), starring Sophia Loren and Marcello Mastroianni. In one of the segments, Loren plays Adelina, who supports herself and her war veteran husband by selling black market cigarettes in postwar Naples. Each time she is arrested she avoids jail because she is pregnant, and the law does not allow a pregnant woman to be incarcerated.

Our yesterday-today-and-tomorrow has something of the same pluck and bravery as Adelina. Every year some of the branches break off, wither, or almost die, and I think this may be the last of it, only to see it once more put forth new little purple leaves. Such a brave flower! I wonder what kind of blossoms it will give us this May on my veranda. 🌿

Yesterday-Today-and-Tomorrow

Summer

SUMMER

16 Japanese Flowering Iris

Iris ensata var. *ensata*

花菖蒲 *hana-shobu*

While the Japanese flowering iris (*hana-shobu*) is one of the traditional decorations for Children's Day, a national holiday celebrated in May, this flower is at its most beautiful in June in most of Japan, under the skies of the first weeks of the rainy season.

Native to Japan, the Japanese flowering iris has been bred selectively by enthusiasts for hundreds of years. Today there are said to be several thousand varieties, which come in a variety of colors and patterns—purple, white, magenta, pink, lilac, yellow, bordered, dappled, and gradated.

In addition to the flowering iris, there are two other species of Japanese iris, *ayame* (Siberian iris), and *kakitsubata* (rabbit-ear iris), and they also bloom when the weather begins to turn hot and humid. To distinguish the flowering iris from the other two species, we look at things like the height of the plant and the size of its flowers; the length and thickness of the leaves; and whether there is a thick vein in the center of the leaf and a streak of yellow at the base of the petal.

Depending on where it was first cultivated, the flowering iris is also divided into types: Ise (Mie Prefecture), Higo (Kumamoto Prefecture), Edo (Tokyo), or Nagai (Yamagata Prefecture). The many different varieties are often named for places, people, or things famous in traditional lore. This is not unknown for other flowers, but the names chosen for the flowering iris seem especially elegant, much like the names for traditional Japanese sweets. Paging through a flower dictionary is a pleasure as one comes across the magenta-tinged "Lord Narihira," whose color resembles the hunting cloak

Japanese Flowering Iris

the medieval poet might himself have worn; the graceful lavender "Sei Shonagon," named for the medieval court lady who wrote *The Pillow Book*; and the pink-tinged "Mademoiselle Yoshino," named after a famed courtesan of the seventeenth century. Then there is the pale magenta "Stone Bridge," which evokes the mythical lions of the eponymous kabuki play; the white with purple border of "River Tatsuta," named for a river in Nara that figures in classical poetry; and "Praising the Sacred Way," a name particularly fitting for a flowering iris of the Ise line, since Ise is the site of the most sacred shrine of Shinto.

When we arrange irises, each school of *ikebana* has its own rules, which vary in strictness and number, and which have been handed down from the heads (*iemoto*) of the different schools to their students. These rules are expressions of the accumulated observations and wisdom of generations about how best to show the beauty of the flowers.

There are schools which take great care with respect to the height and relative position of the flowers, stipulating where they will be facing when fully open, as well as whether the front or back of the leaves will show, how many leaves there are, and even the direction of the leaf tip, which curves ever so slightly, and which is called, at least in our school, the "fingernail."

Ikebana artists emphasize the fresh, green strength and at the same time try to make the elegant and graceful flowers look as beautiful as possible.

Flowering irises under a clear blue sky look quite fresh and lovely, but there is something poignant in the way their fully open petals tremble faintly in the rain. Perhaps the flowering iris has been beloved by the Japanese for so long because of an instinctive attraction to the coexistence of opposites. In its combination of delicacy and strength, I feel it is the quintessential flower of Japan.

Japanese Flowering Iris

17 Hydrangea

Hydrangea macrophylla

紫陽花 *ajisai*

The hydrangea, which is native to Japan, can be traced back to the *gaku ajisai* (*Hydrangea macrophylla* f. *normalis*), of which there are many varieties. All have clusters of small flowers in the blossom's center which make up the actual flower. The sepals around it, which resemble petals, are called ornamental flowers. They form a frame around the flower, hence the Japanese name *gaku ajisai*, which literally means "frame hydrangea." The other Japanese name, "four petals" (*yohira*), also seems apt, since those four petal-like sepals are the basis of the flower's shape.

The Japanese hydrangea was selectively bred for a long time outside of Japan. In the period since the Western hydrangea returned to Japan, after the many changes it underwent there (as suggested by "seven changes," one of its many Japanese names), it has come to adorn flower shops here both as cut flowers and potted plants.

The hydrangea has a variety of manifestations, we are told: blue if the soil in which it is grown is acidic, and reddish, as in Europe, where the soil is more alkaline.

In *ikebana* we try to make use of the lines of the hydrangea even at the beginning of spring, when the young green leaves have just come out. Then when the leaves turn deep green and the buds blossom, we gather the flowers into large bunches and put the branches into a flower container, so the round flower heads seem to float in space. Among them are what we call "autumn colors hydrangea," which add their own shades of blue and purple, various hues of green, or even deep red, to the green leaves. Then, as autumn deepens, the partly

Hydrangea

withered hydrangeas become one of our *ikebana* staples.

Perhaps because the color changes so distinctly, hydrangea are called "fickle," "wicked," and "proud," in the language of flowers, names which make me pity this flower.

The other day I learned that a melody I have known for a long time belonged to a song called "Mademoiselle Hydrangea" (*ajisai musume*, or "Mademoiselle Hortensia" in the original French). The story tells of a thrifty orphan who becomes a rich and splendid countess. The French chanson singer Yvette Girard often sang this happy waltz on her many visits to Japan, a country she loved. Having been here so often, she must have seen the original Japanese hydrangea (*gaku ajisai*). Perhaps the image of the plain Japanese hydrangea transformed into the splendid Western one was in her mind as she sang.

In order to preserve the freshness of the flowers, we cut them in water before arranging them and then tap and break the stems and rub in some burnt alum. (The "hydra" part of the English word "hydrangea" comes from "hydro-," meaning water.) In recent years, new varieties of hydrangea have been bred in the United States, such as oakleaf hydrangea, the autumn-blooming Annabelle hydrangea, the pinkish *minazuki*, and the pyramid hydrangea (a hybrid from the Japanese panicled hydrangea). Their freshness is preserved by the method just described. However, when they are arranged in a transparent glass container, the alum makes the water cloudy, so we arrange them after lightly pounding the cut end so that as many of the plant fibers are in contact with the water as possible.

As the hydrangeas in bloom keep changing their colors here, there, and everywhere, they insert life into this languid, humid season, as if they were trying to perk us all up. Against the background of their slightly pointed green leaves, the blossoms fly vividly into our vision. A kind of time flows through hydrangeas that differs from that of their surroundings.

18 Gardenia

Gardenia jasminoides
栀子 *kuchinashi*

The gardenia, with its boundless whiteness and sweet scent, is most appealing in this season, when its leaves turn a deeper green.

The name of the flower itself brings to mind the American movie *Summertime*, in which Katharine Hepburn plays an American woman nearing middle age on holiday in Venice. Sitting in a café on the Piazza San Marco, she is approached by an Italian man played by Rossano Brazzi. With her unique charm, Hepburn beautifully conveys the subtleties of female feeling as the encounter swiftly escalates into a passionate love affair and then ends after a few days, when she discovers that her lover is married with several children and decides to end the relationship.

Boarding a *vaporetto*, she makes her way via canal to the train station. As the train is about to leave, she looks out the window for one last glimpse at all she is leaving behind—Venice, love, youth— and there, to her surprise and joy, running along the platform, is her lover. Unable to catch up with the train, which is pulling out, he holds up what he has brought for her—a pure white gardenia, which she had told him was her favorite flower. She waves to him with all her heart, and there the movie ends.

There are single-layered gardenias and double-layered ones, but the beautiful whiteness of all varieties turns brown in a single day. And yet for the character in the film, the gardenia's blinding white will never fade. I have not read the original play on which the movie was based, but having the story end with the unforgettable gardenia may have been the idea of the director, David Lean, who also wrote

Gardenia

the film's script, which is of the quality one would expect from the master who gave us such film classics as *Brief Encounter, Lawrence of Arabia, Doctor Zhivago*, and *The Bridge on the River Kwai*.

I have a personal memory associated with the gardenia. Among my oldest friends is a married couple, both textile dyers. Some years ago, at an exhibition devoted entirely to their works in pongee *tsumugi*, I stood before a certain semi-formal kimono for quite some time, transfixed by the delicate layering of its many yellow lines. It was not only the depth of the hues, but the subtly different levels of intensity, which gave off different kinds of light.

"Insects stay away from kimono that have been colored with dye made from gardenia seed pods," the husband told me. His words surprised me, since as a child I once found a big green insect just as I was about to cut a gardenia in our garden and jumped up in alarm. That kimono dyed with gardenia pods was the first one I bought with my own earnings.

Once the gardenia goes to seed, it takes on several new roles. Besides the dyes that discourage insects from feeding on textiles, it is used to color such foods as *kuri kinton*, a special New Year's dish of sweet potatoes and chestnuts, and also as an ingredient in traditional Chinese medicines.

I wonder if David Lean knew that after its flowers are gone, the seeds of the gardenia live on in so many reincarnations. Like Katharine Hepburn, who, after making *Summertime*, appeared in many more movies and lived a long and fruitful life. 🌱

19 Marigold

Tagetes

マリーゴールド *marigorudo*

"My mother-in-law is in good spirits today, so please come and see her. She's in the prayer room." So saying, my friend Indu, a longtime student of *ikebana* in India, led me to a room the size of an elementary school classroom in a building apart from the main house. Her mother-in-law, who was about ninety years old, was sitting in front of a Hindu altar, together with a nurse in a sari. The altar held statues of the gods surrounded by colorful Indian flowers. A great many garlands of yellow and orange marigolds were draped over the statues' necks, together with other flowers of white and red, like multilayered necklaces. It made a spectacular sight. The window was filled with hanging marigold garlands, bending under their own weight in graceful curves.

Indu leaned down and spoke close to her mother-in-law's ear. "Here's a flower teacher, come from Tokyo in Japan!"

Mother turned her nearly blind eyes towards me and beckoned with her hand.

"Is that so? Please come here."

She took something out of a wooden box beside her, which was full of marigold petals, and gestured to me to open my hand, on which she placed some nuts. Then she put some crumpled, ruby-red paper money into my hand. Seeing that I was baffled, Indu explained.

"It's pocket money for you."

The last time I'd received pocket money was so long ago that I can't even remember when it was. I pressed my palms together and touched both index fingers to the tip of my nose in the most

Marigold

respectful greeting.

Next, Mother said, "Please drink this," and held out a small glass containing some liquid. For an instant I did not know what to do.

I was certain that it was water from the holy river Ganges. I knew that this was the most respectful way to welcome a guest so it would be rude not to drink it. I decided that as soon as I had expressed my gratitude and returned to my hotel, I would have to drink the medicine I had brought with me from Japan since, unaccustomed as I was to Indian water, I would probably feel unwell the next day.

Back at the hotel, I turned on the television and discovered that one of my favorite American movies was playing. Without thinking, I lay down to watch, and the next thing I knew it was two o'clock in the morning. I hadn't taken the medicine and nothing had happened.

Marigolds are native to Mexico. One sees French marigolds in flowerbeds, where they are thought to repel nematodes in the soil. The African marigold has been selectively bred and is used as a cut flower. Both the French and the African varieties are strongly scented.

Could the reason I didn't get sick the day after my visit to Indu be the water from the sacred Ganges I had drunk? Or was it the aura created by the strong scent of all the orange and yellow marigolds in that room that protected me?

India seems to have cast a spell on me. I have been there five times now on private trips, and six for business. 🏵

Marigold

20 Japanese Honeysuckle

Lonicera japonica Thunb.

吸葛 *suikazura*

If you walk through the fields from early summer on, you will see twining vines with small white flowers. This is Japanese honeysuckle, "the sipping vine," also known as *nindo*, "winter enduring." Just as the name suggests, its green leaves endure the winter; when its flowers open in early summer, insects flock to it. The flowers are white at first and then turn yellow, which is why it is also called the "gold and silver flower."

Others in this family include trumpet honeysuckle, a red flower which derives its name from its trumpet-like shape and is native to the United States. Neither of these varieties of honeysuckle lasts long once it is cut, but their life can be extended a little if you lightly pound the cut end and apply vinegar to it.

A friend who lives in America told me, "Yes, I have it in my garden, and the bees love it!" You can see where its Japanese name, "the sipping vine," comes from. The English name, "honeysuckle," reminds me of the American song "Honeysuckle Rose," in which a lover calls his sweetheart a honeysuckle rose, saying that even the bees are jealous of him because she is so sweet and her lips taste like honey.

The lyrics are a little corny, but the lilting rhythm takes over, and you cannot help but feel an uncomplicated happiness as you listen. Of course the lyrics also play on the double meaning of "honey"— as a food and as the beloved. But what is the "rose" doing there? I confess it is still a mystery to me, and the botanical dictionary was of no help.

Japanese Honeysuckle

An American friend pointed out that "Rose" is a woman's name, but it seems to me the lyricist just added it for metrical reasons. I like to think of the title itself as someone's name. Honeysuckle Rose makes me think of a sweet-looking girl who entwines her arm with her lover's, like a vine.

In Japan, we have the "Teika vine" (*teika kazura*) or Asiatic jasmine, which evokes the image of the poet Fujiwara Teika in Komparu Zenchiku's medieval Noh play *Teika*. Teika so loved Princess Shikishi that he turned into a vine which wound around her grave. This vine has none of the adorable sweetness we associate with the Japanese honeysuckle.

We also have the "good-looking man vine" (*binan kazura*) or Japanese kadsura, with its red berries in autumn. They say that it was so named because men once used the juice from the berries to groom their hair.

As we see, twining vines have spawned many a tale.

21 Red Currant

Ribes rubrum

赤房酸塊 *akafusasuguri*

At this season, the most interesting cultivated currant is the red currant. If you lift the stalk attached to the underside of the hand-shaped leaves, you will find small berries in different colors, ranging from green to orange to red.

Under the summer sun, the translucent berries take on subtle hues. You may be attracted to them and hold up a cluster to admire, but beware! The clusters attached to the narrow green stalks crush easily, and their thin juice is impossible to remove if it touches your clothing.

In Japanese, the word for currant is written with the characters for "acidic" and "a clump," and indeed the small fruits have a sweet-sour taste. Varieties such as red currant, black currant, white currant, and gooseberries, which are all closely related, bring up memories of jam, candy, juice, dry fruits, and cassis liqueur.

The best known Japanese member of the ribes genus, which includes edible currants, is the hawthorn bush (*yabusanzashi*), which also has red berries in autumn.

The branches of red currant, which are almost completely straight, are sometimes used in *ikebana*. When you see the marvelous contrast between the summery soft green of the leaves and the color of the currants peeping out from among them, you feel that such a sight belongs exclusively to this season of transience.

Well, now, how about an ice cold cassis soda, or, with just a bit more effort, adding champagne to crème de cassis for a Kir Royale, and letting the currant be the start of a summer night's dream?

Red Currant

22 Indian Lotus

Nelumbo nucifera

蓮 *hasu*

Its leaves, its flowers, its fruits, all make good *ikebana* material, and its root and seeds are edible—what more could you ask? The lotus is an unmixed blessing. Buddha sits on a lotus seat, and in Asia this plant traditionally adorns a variety of scenes in painting and sculpture depicting the nobility as well as the common folk. We also know that even in Egypt lotuses existed from ancient times.

Look at the appearance of the rolled-up leaves before they unfurl into roundness. Feel the breeze that blows through the fresh green leaves. Watch the dew that is thrown off and rolls around on the leaves. And listen as people debate the truth or falsity of the claim that the pink and white blossoms, because of their plump shape, create a little popping sound when they open. The lotus never ceases to intrigue and inspire.

The lotus was imported from China to Japan at an early date, then selectively bred to make the root edible, as a food we now call *renkon* or "lotus root." The plant is quite lovely even after the blossoms begin to scatter. In the autumn, the green, central part turns brown and becomes the round and flattish fruit which is made up of many small holes, each holding a single seed. The fruit looks much like a honeycomb, and in fact the origin of *hasu*, or lotus, in Japanese, is, we are told, *hachisu*, literally, "bee's nest."

The candied lotus seeds that travelers to Taiwan and Hong Kong bring home with them are sweet, but not only that. What makes them delicious is the slight tang of the lotus seeds themselves. And when you infuse lotus flower tea from Vietnam in hot water, the

Indian Lotus

fragile fragrance of the flower floats up to your nostrils. Take a sip and an indescribably delicate flavor fills your mouth, inducing a state of pure relaxation.

In 1951, Dr. Ichiro Ohga discovered two-thousand-year-old lotus seeds in the city of Chiba. He was able to make one of them germinate the next year, and it produced a single pink blossom. People were astounded at the life force of the lotus. But for all its hardiness, if you cut the lotus leaf off at the root, it stops taking in water and wilts. The pink water lily (*suiren*) and the yellow cow lily (*ko-hone*) do likewise if cut in the same manner.

That is why there is a special technique for making these plants draw in water. Water (or a liquid extract of tobacco, as was once the case) is placed in a special, small pump and quickly injected into the stalk. (Tobacco stimulates the stalk's ability to take in water.) Place the surface of the leaf downward; make an incision in the stalk and push it firmly into the pump; and watch the underside of the leaf as the water runs from the center towards the edges through the veins of the leaf, as if they were blood vessels, with the color of the leaf changing in a radial fashion.

While doing this, however, there is one thing you must be careful of in the case of the lotus leaf. You must insert the water from the bottom, while the leaf is turned downwards and firmly press up with your finger on the hole in the center of the leaf (the so-called "belly-button," to *ikebana* practitioners). Failing that, water will spray out in a kind of mist and then spurt strongly upwards. Saturated, you will find yourself the unintended personification of the old metaphor for youthful beauty—a (very) "dewy woman" or "man." 🌱

Indian Lotus

23 Blackberry Lily

Iris domestica

檜扇 *hiogi*

In Japanese, the blackberry lily is called "cypress fan" (*hiogi*), probably because its leaves, before it buds, resemble a fully opened fan made of Japanese hinoki cypress. Such fans have a long history in Japan, chiefly at the imperial court.

The flat, thick leaves rise singly from the base upwards, overlapping a little. Each is twisted very slightly.

In summer, stalks emerge from between the powdery leaves, and, as they branch off, yellow-orange flowers with speckles at the center appear at the tips. One after another, the blooms open up, followed by plump, light green seed pods.

In *ikebana* we often use the ornamental varieties, especially the *daruma* blackberry lily, so named for the somehow humorous shape of its fruit, which resembles one of the small, round Daruma dolls (modeled after Bodhidharma, the founder of Zen Buddhism) that some people keep for good luck. When its flowers are gone, we can still enjoy the sight of its fresh green pods or seed capsules.

This pale green capsule gradually turns amber-colored, then dries and bursts. After that, firm, black, seed-like berries, called *nubatama* or *ubatama*, form in the center. In classical Japanese poetry, *nubatama* is one of the most common epithets (*makura-kotoba*) for anything black or very dark, but I was unfamiliar with any discussion of its substantive origin. Here is the real thing, I thought. Taking a few berries in my hand, I examined them closely.

I often receive presents of traditional Japanese sweets whose names include *nubatama*. They are typically blackish in color, and

Blackberry Lily

some are made with very dark brown sugar. Since I knew *nubatama* as a poetic epithet, I had always assumed that the names for these sweets were allusions to classical poetry, but now that I had seen the actual *nubatama* berries themselves, I had a new sense of the names of these sweets, quite vivid and concrete.

The color black is not unusual in the world of plants. However, almost all that appear black, like the black lily, actually contain purple or red tints as well. When it comes to berries, though, even if they are green at first, there are many which turn almost black when ripe.

As autumn nears, pokeweed berries, for example, turn black, ripen, and fall to the ground. If you step on them, or if the juice gets on your clothes, the color is impossible to remove. Japanese privet berries are a very dark, charcoal gray. Honeysuckle berries turn dark purple or almost black when they ripen. Since there is an unlimited number of berries that are almost black in color, I wonder why the ancient poets chose those of the blackberry lily as a metaphor for blackness.

Could it be because of the lacquer-like luster on the round surface of the berries, which gives their blackness such depth? Or might it be because there was no other berry as black as that at the time the need for such a metaphor first arose? Thus the blackberry lily poses yet another riddle.

Blackberry Lily

24 Hibiscus

Hibiscus

ハイビスカス *haibisukasu*

What makes people gravitate to this flower? Perhaps it is its bright and sunny colors and the unique long peduncle which emerges from the center of the flower. Hibiscus comes in a variety of colors— red, yellow, orange, pink, white. Sometimes the center color is more intense, sometimes there are subtle gradations of color, and sometimes the petals may be multilayered. The length of the stamen differs depending on the angle of the flower and its variety. In the case of the coral hibiscus of Zanzibar (the island in the Indian Ocean), the long flower peduncle hangs straight down, with a stamen that calls to mind a wind chime.

As we know it today in Japan, the hibiscus flower originally came from cross-fertilization of several species of the hibiscus genus, including the Chinese hibiscus. Even if cut from a garden or a pot, the thin petals lose their beauty in less than a day. No matter how much you water the flowers, it is impossible to extend their life by more than a few hours. The rose of sharon, the cotton rosemallow, and the brilliant hibiscus are all members of the hibiscus family, as is shown by their botanical names (*hibiscus syriacus, hibiscus mutabilis,* and *hibiscus coccineus,* respectively), so naturally they have properties in common with the hibiscus flower.

The hibiscus, we are told, came from Okinawa to Japan sometime during the Edo period. How rare and wonderful this flower, with its air of the south, must have seemed to the ruler at that time, and then, eventually, to ordinary people.

These days the hibiscus is the most popular flower on the aloha

Hibiscus

shirt, and poolside it blossoms even on the liveliest swimsuits, stirring up a longing for tropical lands. A number of varieties of ornamental hibiscuses were bred in Hawaii, and it has become the state flower.

Hibiscus comes in intense colors, yet the flower, strangely enough, does not give the impression of being at odds with its surroundings. Rather it seems to melt into the background, creating a sense of easy intimacy. When its petals flutter in the breeze on a hot day, the temperature seems to drop.

We get through the heat of summer sipping healthy hibiscus tea. By mid-August the artificial hibiscus that is a component of department store décor at the morale-boosting summer sales disappears. Eventually pots of the real thing quietly vanish from flower shops, too. Once again it seems that summer has gone by in a flash, without time for a proper vacation, without one even being possible, and we have not fully enjoyed it. At such times, the hibiscus seems to embody the spirit of lost summer for the Japanese. 🌺

25 Hollyhock

Alcea rosea
立葵 *tachiaoi*

Hollyhock blooms from the bottom up, beginning from the base of the flower's tall, fuzzy stalk. Sometimes the stalk reaches the height of a person or higher. The flowers, which are on the large side, can be pink, white, pale yellow, red, or magenta, some single, and some fully double. In early summer, no other flowering plant blooms as lushly.

It is during the rainy season that hollyhocks come into bloom, and as the season draws to a close, most of them fade away under the strong sun. For this reason, they are also referred to as "rainy season hollyhocks." However, since their timetable depends on their geographical location and the weather, some do bloom on into late summer.

Unlike the dynamic sunflower, the hollyhock has an aura of gentleness and gaiety. And yet it does not have a noble image. The flowers are attached to the stem almost at right angles, like megaphones. It was brought to Japan in the pre-Muromachi period (1336-1573), and nowadays it grows wild in the regions where the climate stays hot all year around. I'd love to see it gaily blossoming there.

In Japan, you often encounter the hollyhock in unexpected places. If you pay attention, you can glimpse its high spires rising from cracks in the asphalt of old parking lots, or towering above the grass. On the roadside above the moat of the Imperial Palace in Tokyo, the eyes of passersby are drawn to the tall hollyhocks with their colorful blooms. The appearance of the buds during the rainy season and early summer is a reminder to the caretakers who groom the grounds to be careful and not to cut them down along with the weeds.

Once I was on a trip in the early summer, and, at the edge of a bright green rice field, I saw a row of hollyhocks encircling a farmhouse. I thought about how the family who lived in the house must enjoy caring for them and how their neighbors must look forward to their coming into bloom each year, too.

One way to keep hollyhocks fresh is to cut them and then immediately burn the cut part and place them in deep water. Even so, the flowers wither quickly. This flower does best when it is allowed to bloom freely in nature. And yet, although the flowers vanish before you know it, the round fruits with their seeds inside follow soon after.

I have a summer kimono of cream-colored silk patterned with white hollyhocks that I had been keeping for the right occasion. This year I finally had a chance to wear it, but it was the hottest day of the year, when no one would typically wear a kimono. I felt a little awkward in it, but I was able to hold myself up straight and walk with head held high, as if in tandem with my kimono's statuesque hollyhocks. 🌼

Hollyhock

Autumn

AUTUMN

26 Bush Clover

Lespedeza
萩 *hagi*

I was gloomily walking along in the glare of the late summer sun, when beside the path, I noticed some bush clover with several small flowers.

> Bush clover, silvergrass,
> kudzu flowers, fringed pinks,
> golden lace, and also
> thoroughwort flowers and
> the morning glories
> *Yamanoue Okura*

This well-known poem from the *Man'yoshu* lists the "seven grasses of autumn," which are actually flowering plants. Bush clover is the first to be mentioned, but that may be less for the sake of rhythm than because of the Japanese fondness for this plant since at least the poet Okura's time. In the *Man'yoshu*, bush clover appears in 140 poems, more than any other plant.

Bush clover, which is native to Japan, is a hardy plant which can adapt to a variety of soils and climates. Like other members of the pea family in shape, its flowers resemble a butterfly. The color is most often fuchsia, but sometimes on one bush there may be crimson-violet and white, or variegated flowers resembling tie-dyed fabric. Then there is white bush clover, whose white coloring evokes a feeling of coolness.

Bush Clover

In Japan, you may see bush clover branches dangling down with their many small flowers, the whole bush swaying in the breeze. Or people cheerfully passing through a bush clover tunnel and finding the petals scattered profusely over the ground when they happen to look down at their feet. Such sights as these make me feel that the bush clover has nothing pushy about it but that in any landscape it is a gentle presence that can live in harmony with any other plant.

As a young girl, I once had a tutor for English who came from a prestigious family and made an arranged marriage in her third year of college. One day her mother-in-law told her to pick some bush clover from the garden and arrange it in a bamboo basket. "You have a diploma in *ikebana*," said the mother-in-law, "so you should be able to do it."

What the young bride did not know was this: even if you carry a bucket to where the bush clover flowers are growing and place them in water as soon as you cut them, having first swiftly pounded the base and swabbed them with alcohol, they fade almost at once. That is why florists do not stock them. The young woman began her arrangement, but it was impossible to make the flowers hold a shape and soon they were wilting, as much from their own nature as from the heat of her hands as she worked with them. And then there were the tears that spilled over onto the back of those same hands.

My heart skipped a beat when I heard this story from my mother. I was a junior high school student and did not take my lessons in *ikebana* at all seriously, but I thought to myself that this was one of the difficulties that would await me if I got married, so I had better put more effort into my lessons. Looking back, I feel that bush clover may indeed be one of the underlying factors in my decision to make *ikebana* my life's work. Bush clover gives an impression of being docile and gentle, but it can surprise you with its willfulness. 🌾

27 Balloon Vine

Cardiospermum halicacabum

風船葛 *fusenkazura*

Were I asked to choose a plant to grow as a green curtain to mitigate the summer heat in Tokyo, I daresay I would choose the balloon vine over the more usual choices of bitter melon and morning glories.

Unlike bitter melon, we don't eat it, and, unlike morning glories, it has no beautiful flowers; yet its pale green "balloons" set this plant apart in a most appealing way. Swaying lightly in the breeze, it gives off an aura of refreshing charm. As the shoots grow, the tendrils at the base of the leaves clamber up towards the frame about which they will twine. They grow to more than twice the height of a person, sometimes much more.

The white flowers themselves are tiny and come into bloom at summer's end. When the flowers die, pods with seeds inside emerge. At the tips of the narrow shoots, they respond airily to every breeze. The puffy pods, in light green, are two to three centimeters in diameter (about one inch) and have three raised edges. The temptation to crush one is strong, but try to wait until they turn the color of amber. When they make a faint rustling sound as they are shaken, then open them up. The seeds inside are round, and there is a white, heart-shaped mark on their pure black surface where they were attached to the pod. Another name for balloon vine is "heart pea," which seems quite apt.

When we arrange balloon vine, we take almost all the leaves off and roll the green vines up or, alternately, leave them to cascade richly down from a tall vase or container in their natural state. The balloon vine is regal looking, and yet something about it is uncivi-

Balloon Vine

lized too. It goes well with any other flower material, but, when you twist the vines around other plants, or let its pods play in space, its barely there weight catches the air where it stops, and, as it floats suspended, your sense of the space is completely changed. No matter how you arrange it, though, the overall impression is always one of lightness, and so the balloon vine lives up to its name.

Balloon Vine

28 Great Burnet

Sanguisorba officinalis
吾亦紅 *waremoko*

Autumn was in the air when I travelled to Hokkaido in early August. The fields were aglow with flowers. Plumes were beginning to appear atop the silver *susuki* grass, while the golden lace, red grass, balloon flowers or Chinese balloon flowers, and fringed pinks were in full bloom. In amongst them, the small, elliptical-shaped burnet flowers peeked out here and there.

Any mention of the "seven grasses of autumn," which are actually flowering plants, brings to mind the poem by Yamanoue Okura discussed earlier in "Bush Clover" (Chapter 26). Some of the plants I was looking at in Hokkaido are listed in that poem, but not the burnet.

The history of the burnet flower is unexpectedly long, with the flower making an appearance as far back as the "Niou no Miya" chapter of *The Tale of Genji* (early eleventh century). Perhaps it did not yet exist in the seventh or eighth century, during Yamanoue Okura's lifetime, or, possibly, because it thrives at comparatively high elevations, he never saw one. Or, perhaps he did see it, but it seemed rather dull and did not appeal to him. Even in the *Tale of Genji* it was described as "the plain-looking burnet."

The green stalk of the burnet paired with its dark red flower is quite elegant. Yet the stalk breaks easily, and it is delicate work to remove the small jagged leaves that grow along its length so as to achieve a clean, uncluttered line. Many small flowers grow outward all along the stalk, so if you want to arrange them in a way that looks as if they are floating in space, you must consider how best

Great Burnet

to thin them out.

Unlike the "seven grasses of spring," which are actually herbs and wild vegetables we think of as foods to nourish us, the flowering plants that we call the "seven grasses of autumn" are strictly for ornamental use. Compared to other autumn plants, the burnet has a rather unusual color and shape. If you combine several stalks you can create an unexpectedly large space of definite individuality. At the same time, even a single flowering stalk can add depth to the final work.

> In the autumn fields
> the flowers are in bloom—
> counting on my fingers, one by one
> I find the flowers of
> the seven grasses

This *Man'yoshu* poem by an unknown poet is followed by Okura's poem naming each of the flowering plants of autumn one by one, almost as if he were echoing and affirming: "Yes, there are seven, look! There's this one, and that one, and that one and those over there, too."

Sometimes, in arranging flowers, you keep trying to imagine the end result and ask yourself, "How will it look if I place this one next?" or "What if I add a burnet there?" These two poems suggest that we can also arrange flowers in a rather different, more spontaneous, manner.

Were I asked to enumerate the "seven grasses of autumn" for our contemporary age, I would put the burnet first.

29 Plumed Cockscomb

Celosia argentea

鶏頭 *keito*

Cockscomb flowers have existed in Japan from ancient times and even appear in the *Man'yoshu* and other old texts. There they are called *kara-ai*, or "foreign indigo," and historical records tell of their use as a dye.

In modern Japanese, the word for this flower, *keito,* literally means "cockscomb," the jagged red crest that crowns a rooster's head. Indeed, it does resemble a rooster's cockscomb in shape and texture, and its names in English, French, German, Spanish, and Italian all make the same connection.

We tend to think of the cockscomb as an autumn flower, but the Kurume cockscomb (*Celosia argentea* var. *cristata* Kurume Group) is already beginning to bloom in early summer. Its ruffled red and orange heads, made up of many small, plump flowers, are perched atop stiff, straight stalks.

Another variety of cockscomb, commonly called "celosia" in Japanese, is a cultivar that was selectively bred from wild cockscombs. Its long, narrow flower heads have blossoms that are dark pink at the top and then fade to pale pink, with the bottom of the stalk gradually turning the color of platinum. "Celosia" is also, by the way, the botanical name for the whole cockscomb genus itself.

Spiked cockscomb (*yarigeito*, botanical name *Celosia cristata* var. *childsii*) is distinguished by its narrow, pointy shape, like an elongated triangle. Feather cockscomb (*umogeito*, botanical name *Celosia argentea* var. *cristata* Plumosa Group) is quite bushy, and, when it grows tall, looks a little like a shrub. Although both of these varieties

Plumed Cockscomb

are cockscombs, they seem quite tame compared to the intensity and strength of the crested cockscomb (*tosakageito*, botanical name *Celosia argentea* var. *cristata*).

The stalk of the crested cockscomb is flat and sometimes, as we say in *ikebana*, "petrified," while the flower heads look like clusters of wrinkled folds, which in large specimens suggest the structure of a brain. If you cut the flowering stalk from the bottom, the attached leaves will wilt at once, so we remove them with a clean decisive stroke from the stalk. Then you can enjoy the flowers for some time even without water.

At exhibitions these days you sometimes see a crested cockscomb taller than a human being. Among the other flower materials on display, these large flowers in yellow, red, magenta, pink, orange, and light green have a prominent individuality. Eventually, small black particles begin dropping from them, though from where exactly it is difficult to tell. Sometimes they are mistaken for bugs, and people leap to remove them.

In fact, these small black particles are seeds, an emblem of life. Unless it makes a plethora of seeds each year and spreads them around, the perennial plant faces extinction as its fate. As I contemplate this fact, the animal appearance of this plant with its rooster-like cockscomb takes hold of me. Just before it faces its own end, as its seeds come spilling down, I seem to hear the flower crying out, "Attention must be paid!" 🌿

Plumed Cockscomb

30 Silvergrass

Miscanthus sinensis

薄・芒 *susuki*

Silvergrass, which is called *obana* or *susuki* in Japanese, is one of the "seven grasses of autumn" and native to Japan. Its leaves are mostly green, but among the cultivars are zebra grass (*takanoha susuki*, hawk-wing silvergrass) with its pale yellow horizontal bands, and eulalia "variegatus" (*shima susuki*, striped silvergrass) with its vertical stripes. A plant of many faces, silvergrass begins as feathery plumes standing proudly erect, but gradually the seed heads begin to droop, rippling in the wind, until at last they fade away.

In October of 2012, after some workshops I held for our school's branch in Rome, the Japanese Embassy there contacted me to ask if I would provide *ikebana* arrangements for a dinner party they were organizing to promote Japanese food. When I am abroad and creating a proper *ikebana* arrangement using indigenous plant materials, of the three *ikebana* elements—line, color, and mass—it is line, when all is said and done, that is the most essential. Aided by the Italian gardener, who had served under eleven Japanese ambassadors, I gathered several sorts of branches in the garden of the embassy residence. I also found a large clump of silvergrass and cut a bundle of the tall, plumed stalks and wrapped them at once in newspaper to keep the leaves from curling up. Then, I cut the bottoms off and soaked them in vinegar for ten seconds to preserve their freshness.

The dinner was to take place at a villa of the Borghese family, now a private club for former nobles. I was warned several times that taking photographs of the interior was strictly forbidden. The

Silvergrass

sun was beginning to set over Rome as I entered the high-ceilinged, echoing room on the second floor, carrying my flower materials. What attracted my attention at once—even more than the splendid furnishings and the very large, low-hanging chandelier, which I had been asked to be careful of as I worked—was a portrait directly in front of me. I could not take my eyes off the figure painted on the huge canvas. Dressed in a white *haori* coat and *hakama* divided skirt, and with his hair done up in a samurai topknot, the subject of the portrait had to be Japanese. Painters outside Japan tend to give Japanese subjects narrow eyes, but the man in this portrait had round eyes. He seemed to be using them to stare straight towards me.

"It's a portrait of Hasekura Tsunenaga, said to have been painted while he was staying in Rome," said the embassy's cultural attaché, who accompanied me. I knew about Hasekura Tsunenaga, of course, but to find his portrait here was completely unexpected.

Four hundred years ago, Hasekura Tsunenaga departed from Tsukinoura near Ishinomaki for Mexico. Afterwards, as the leader of the Keicho-era (1596-1615) mission to Europe, he went on to Spain and Rome. But why was his portrait in this building? The striking design of his *hakama*, festooned with grassy plants in green and gold on a ground of white, reminded me that it was the daimyo Daté Masamune who had ordered the mission, the same Daté Masamune who was renowned for the daring and beautiful designs of his own apparel and other possessions.

At any rate, in half an hour the former nobles would be gathering for cocktails. Time to stop such musings and arrange the flowers! Some of my students had come from Japan and Europe with their husbands, and we worked together, framing Hasekura's portrait on either side with bamboo and flowers, just as if they were offered in tribute to it. We arranged the many silvergrass plumes with care, so as not to cut our hands on the sharp leaf edges. Thanks to the line made by the leaves, the silvergrass imparted a delicate motion to the work.

The chef's sudden request for a table arrangement as well came after we had already used all the available flower containers. The embassy staff rushed to get a lacquer tray no longer in use from the ambassador's residence. I filled it with water, in which I floated some gold foil that I had brought with me from Japan, thinking it might come in handy at some point. Then I lay silvergrass on the surface of the water and, after cutting off the stalks of some chrysanthemums, added those too.

This past year, there happened to be a television special about Daté Masamune. As soon as I switched the program on, I was transfixed. There on the screen was the letter that Daté Masamune himself had written to the pope and entrusted to Hasekura Tsunenaga. Embedded in the paper, underlying the words Masamune had written, were flecks of gold foil and faded silver. The box which held the letter was black lacquer, decorated with a bold design of peonies and arabesques, and, though the lines were thin, what was clearly silvergrass sprinkled with dew.

A paper tag brown with time, which must have been affixed later on, was attached to the box. In the brief instant that it showed on the screen, I was able to read it. It said "Borghese." No room for doubt: the box was the property of the Borghese family.

Although there are many Borghese residences, the one where I had arranged the flowers was the Villa Borghese itself, in the center of Rome. When I contacted the cultural attaché, he explained, "Pope Paul V was pope when Hasekura Tsunenaga came to Italy and since he was a member of the Borghese family, it is very possible that the letter box belonged to his family."

Hasekura Tsunenaga, having been baptized, later returned to Japan, but by that time Christianity had been banned. He is supposed to have died in his early fifties, a disappointed man. However, there is a theory that he lived on in seclusion for another thirty years. Might the fact that three places claim his grave be evidence for this?

When he was in Europe, Hasekura Tsunenaga must have looked at the world around him with an irrepressible curiosity. Would that explain why the artist who painted his portrait had the impression his eyes were round? Or was it possible, I wondered, speculating with free-wheeling abandon, that for several hundred years no one had presented *ikebana* to the Tsunenaga in the painting and his eyes were registering his surprise?

When the plumes of silvergrass age and start to wither, it seems appropriate to write its Japanese name with 芒, a character that combines the meanings of "grass" and "to die." But for the silvergrass I saw painted in gold on that letter box there will be no withering. It will be treasured and live on as it is, now and forever.

My experience in Rome made me want to know more about Hasekura Tsunenaga, his lord Daté Masamune, and the times they lived in. I had the feeling that Hasekura Tsunenaga was sending me a message—one that took four hundred years to arrive.

Somewhat later I learned that the plants embroidered on the costume in the portrait were also silvergrass. Since then, I cannot help feeling that Hasekura Tsunenaga was making his strong preference for silvergrass felt through me when I chose the flower material that evening at the Villa Borghese. 🌾

31 Glory Lily

Gloriosa

グロリオーサ *guroriosa*

The glory lily comes in several colors, deep orange, a deep pink-ish-red with a yellow border, lemon yellow, or white with just a little pink mixed in.

It is a distinctly showy flower, both because of the brightness of its hues and also the shape of its backward bending petals when it opens. The petals gradually uncurl, but since they are wavy break off easily. Caution is required in working with them, and also in working with the stalk. The leaf tips are tendril-like and intertwine. When creating an arrangement, you will run into problems if you hold in your hand several stalks of the glory lily at the same time. They twist and tangle around one another, and it is extremely difficult to separate them.

Once the flowers bloom, they open wide, and several stamens protrude from the center. The pollen on their tips is a real nuisance, for it will never come off your clothes if it makes contact and you do not remove it correctly. (The way to do it is to wrap Scotch Tape around your hand and lightly brush the cloth surface first. The pollen will stick to the tape instead of becoming deeply enmeshed in the fibers.)

I once had a student who had returned to Japan after living in Europe for several decades, including the last seven years in Spain, and was preparing for her first participation in an *ikebana* exhibition in Japan. During one of our classes she picked up a glory lily that was about eighty centimeters (thirty inches) high, and exclaimed, "How I look forward to using glory lilies with long stems like this

Glory Lily

in the upcoming exhibition! You almost never see them in Spain."

At a flower market in Switzerland I saw the flowers cut so that they were only about twenty-five centimeters (ten inches) high and then placed singly or in pairs in transparent, puffed-up bags before being sold. That may have been to avoid tangling, thus making them easier to handle for both seller and buyer. At the same market, they were also selling glory lilies of about sixty centimeters (two feet) that were not bundled in bags.

I'll never forget the gasp that escaped the audience at a demonstration one time in Japan, when several glory lilies about two meters (six feet) high made their entrance on the stage. It was the first time I had seen such tall glory lilies myself, and I leaned forward eagerly, watching the flowers being positioned one after the other. As each glory lily was arranged in the large container, its long stalk curved into an undulating wave beneath the weight of its flower. When the arrangement was finished, the flowers sitting aloft looked for all the world like yellow butterflies paused to rest.

The person who grew those flowers was not trying to grow long-stalked glory lilies for the sake of novelty alone: they were well aware of the deceptive resilience, and beauty, of the glory lily's long limbs with their gentle upward camber. I realized that this spectacle could never have been realized with short glory lilies like those my student had worked with while abroad.

The glory lily is native to Africa and tropical Asia. In Japan, it can only be cultivated indoors in hothouses, but, even so, I thought, as long as there are growers who have such deep empathy for the sensibility of those who arrange flowers, the joys of *ikebana* will never come to an end. 🌱

32 Sword Bean

Canavalia gladiata

鉈豆 *natamame*

One day I received a heavy package wrapped in a thick paper bag. The address label identified it as a "plant" and the return address was that of a former student. Four or five years ago, he had been in a class I used to meet with once every two months at our school's main branch in Osaka.

Swiftly opening it, I discovered several beans, green in color, dangling from a splendid sword bean vine. There was a note enclosed as well, which said, "The sword bean vine you gave me has grown up." (In Japanese, the name is *natamame*, which means "billhook bean," because it makes you think of a billhook.)

That's right, I had taken some sword bean plants left over from an exhibition in Tokyo once to Osaka. At the end of one of the classes, I offered them to anyone who wanted to try their hand at cultivating them, and several people took me up on the offer. I think I heard a year or so later from a few of them—"One grew for me," or "We have two now"—but I hadn't thought about the plants for a long time. Looking at the splendid sword bean plant I received in the mail was like seeing an adult child come home with my grandchild and great-grandchild. I sat down at once to write a thank you letter.

Compared to an ordinary bean, the sword bean is quite large. Perhaps that is because it continues to grow inside the pod. It is also heavy in the hand, yet less thick than you would expect from the weight. And then there are the pods, which can be nearly forty centimeters (fifteen inches) in length, and whose curved lines add interest to a flower arrangement. You can use the sword bean in

Sword Bean

its natural state, with its fresh green color and the beans dangling down, or you can use it when dried. Then both the beans and the vines are a pale yellow, and the plant is attractive in a different way. Some years back I was asked to decorate the first floor window of a department store in Tokyo. Instead of placing the stalk in water, I let the plant dry out, painted it gold, and hung it up. In spite of myself, I could not help admiring the sight of the golden beans dangling from the golden vine.

The sword bean plays a role in daily life, including in food. The red sword bean (*aka natamame*) is used in *fukujinzuke*, a kind of crunchy pickle often eaten with Japanese-style curry.

Just now, shaking a sword bean pod that had dried out the year before last, and hearing its rattle, I realized I was holding a musical instrument. A maraca, maybe. I'll paint a picture on it one of these days and it will be one of a kind.

Ideas and images spiral out endlessly from the sword bean vine.

33 Withered Sunflower

Helianthus annuus

枯向日葵 *kare-himawari*

Withered Indian lotus, withered *susuki* silvergrass, withered Japanese banana leaf: these are what we observe as autumn deepens and they return to the earth, frail remnants of the robust plants they were at peak bloom time, filling us with a sense of desolation.

I once arranged withering sunflower for an *ikebana* demonstration on the island of Cyprus. At two meters (six and a half feet) high, it was much taller than I, and its thick stalk, about four centimeters (an inch and a half) in diameter, was completely bare of leaves and yellow petals. When I picked it up, I found that the head, where the seeds were packed in so tightly, was not completely dry, and I stumbled under the heavy weight. As I carried it on stage, the round head rolled comically.

The shape of each seed at the center of the sunflower becomes very clear when the flower dries out. It changes appearance so drastically that you find you can no longer recognize the flower head and associate it with the dramatic and forceful image of the golden yellow summer bloom. It is as if this plant, nourished in the earth with water and light from the heavens, is gradually stripped of superfluities and squeezed to its essence.

The round center looks as though it has been turned inside out and crushed, and there are gaps in the seeds. It reminds me of a face. You almost wonder if this plant, which started off the season as a friend to the sun, is open and bright only in summer—and whether its jaundiced, fall expression represents its true nature. Each seed develops at a different rate, and it may be these small differences in

Withered Sunflower

the timing of their development that create the wavy shape of the total surface. The countless seeds have a contemporary look with their striped surface. They can be made into a nutritious, edible oil.

Gazing at the gaps that remain when the ripened seeds fall, we get a glimpse of the emptiness left behind as new lives set forth on their travels. We look into the profound world that belongs to the sunflower alone.

Vincent van Gogh painted seven sunflower canvases, showing them at their peak, but also just before they began to wilt. I cannot help wondering what a completely dried sunflower would have looked like had he painted one.

Sofu Teshigahara, founder of the Sogetsu School of Ikebana, made the observation in his *Kadensho* (*Book of Flowers*) that "withered things are beautiful, drooping things are not."

The more the sunflower withers, the more individual it becomes. It stands before us with a new boldness and daring, different now from when it bloomed so proudly, as if to say, "Did you think I would be one of those that merely droops?"

34

Oriental (Japanese) Bittersweet

Celastrus orbiculatus

蔓梅擬 *tsuruumemodoki*

It was late autumn one year, just before Halloween, I think, when my work took me to Canada and the eastern United States.

At the open-air market in Ottawa, I saw Japanese bittersweet, with the new seeds in their orange-yellow coats peeking out from the bursting berries. I wondered if they were used for Halloween decorations, which are usually black and orange. Compared to the bittersweet I was used to seeing in Japan, these made me want to shake some life into them, tell them to straighten up. Barely a meter (three feet) long, they drooped listlessly and there was no strength in their contour. Their natural line, vibrant and lively as a single brushstroke drawn in one fell swoop, such as we see in Japan, was entirely absent. In *ikebana*, we display this plant with the branches coiled up or unroll them and let them dangle down. Too much length might have been the problem with the bittersweet I saw in that market in Ottawa, which would have made it difficult to carry home, let alone work with. It looked to me as if they had merely cut the tips off the wobbly branches.

Oriental bittersweet grows primarily in Japan so its appearance abroad is fairly recent. Perhaps it is valued there chiefly as a colorful display in autumn. In Japan, we regard it as a vine, and its name, *tsuruumemodoki*, means "the winterberry (*umemodoki*)-like vine."

Oriental (Japanese) Bittersweet

It grows by twining itself around other plants or even itself. It must be unwound before it can be taken to the flower market, so it is rather difficult to procure the vines in their original length (which is something I have always wanted to see, wondering how many ways there are to arrange it so that its length and curves show to the best effect). Perhaps the bittersweet I saw in Ottawa had been growing wild, and someone had just gathered up an armful.

The berries of the Oriental bittersweet, with its winding vines, are yellowish green at first, but when they ripen, they gradually turn almost pure yellow. At this time, there is still a certain heaviness to the vines. But when you strip off some of the berries in order to show off the vine's contour, the branches become lighter and spring into the air. The balance has changed. The berries still have some moisture in them and are not completely dried out. When they are fully ripe, the skins burst and divide into three, and orange-coated seeds emerge from the center. Peek inside the broken flesh, see the fresh yellow against the orange of the seeds, and you will behold the essence of autumn abundance. At this point, rather than putting the vines in a container with water, I am tempted to fully expose their beauty by arranging them so that they are suspended from a height. Unfortunately, the berries shed so much skin when they burst that you end up constantly having to sweep them up.

Someone I know was determined to grow Oriental bittersweet in her garden and asked me to help her find some. I was unable to find a plant at a flower shop in the city, so I asked a florist I knew in the country. He delivered two plants, and, when I thanked him, he said, "You will need a male and a female with this plant, you know."

In other words, Oriental bittersweet is a dioecious plant. Unless you have both a female and a male plant, the vine will not bear fruit. The flowers of the male are green, and the female pale yellow. Oriental bittersweet has its own quiet charm when in flower, which differs from its bright beauty in autumn when the berries burst.

35 Myrtle

Myrtus communis
ミルト *miruto*

My first encounter with myrtle occurred in Rome in October 2012. There was a series of events there, some of which involved the Japanese Embassy, and I was asked to arrange the flowers for them with materials from the embassy gardens. The head gardener, who was Italian, was of great help to me in gathering the plants. The day after the final event, when I was holding a flower-arranging seminar at a hotel outside the city, he unexpectedly appeared bearing several plants, all wrapped in paper, and presented them to me saying, "You may not have these in Japan. I thought you might like to use them in your seminar."

One of them had lustrous green leaves and blue-black berries that made an unforgettable impression. He told me it was called myrtle, or *mirto* in Italian, and that it grew all over the Mediterranean, especially on the island of Sardinia, where they macerate the blue-black fruit with sugar to make a homemade digestif they also call *mirto*. Before I could tell him how grateful I was, he hopped back on his motorbike and zoomed off, saying, "I'm spending my day off with my family but have a good trip and see you again someday!"

I wondered about the identity of this plant whose branches bend under the weight of its dark-colored berries. When I got back to Japan I looked it up. Lo and behold, its Japanese name was *ginka ume*, *ginko bai*, or *ginbaika*, "silver fragrant plum" or "silver plum flower."

I had used *ginbaika* in *ikebana* arrangements on a few occasions. It has narrow, elliptical leaves, which are slightly pointed at the tips.

Myrtle

But I have never seen the variety with berries in Japan. The photograph of myrtle in the botanical dictionary shows a small, pretty flower with pure white petals and a long, protruding white stamen. Sometimes called "the celebration tree," it is also used as a decoration at weddings. The dictionary also remarks on its strong life force and says that it is used as an herb.

The great German writer Goethe crossed the Brenner Pass in 1780 and entered what is now Italy. Enchanted by the bright Italian light, he journeyed all the way south to Sicily. In his later *Wilhelm Meister's Apprenticeship*, he captured his memories of the trip in "Mignon's Song," in which he mentions myrtle. The first verse goes like this:

> Do you know the land where
> citron trees blossom and
> golden fruits ripen in dark forests
> weighing down the branches,
> while from clear azure skies soft breezes blow
> among peaceful myrtle and soaring laurel trees?
> To there, to there, with me you must go, o my beloved!

Myrtle comes originally from along the coastline of the Mediterranean, where the soil, air, water, and light are unique to that geographical location. This is the plant that the embassy's head gardener made that special trip to give me, and the plant that Goethe's poem extolls. It is not identical to the *ginbaika*, which grows in Japan. A plant needs its native soil to grow. And so I dream. Of someday, being under the blossoming citron trees, sipping *mirto*, caressed by the soft breezes of southern Italy. 🌱

36 Japanese Beautyberry

Callicarpa japonica
紫式部 *murasakishikibu*

When I think of purplish berries and fruits, I think of blueberries, dark purple Kalamata olives, the purplish-blue berries of Indian poke, and the bright blue berries of mondo grass. But none of these have quite the hue of the Japanese beautyberry. This elegant plant, with the delicate lines of its branches and its small, round berries, is called *murasaki shikibu* in Japanese, after Murasaki Shikibu, the elegant court lady of medieval Japan who wrote *The Tale of Genji*. Its leaves grow in pairs from opposite sides of the twigs, and the leaf margins are finely serrated. In early summer, small, pale lavender flowers bloom in clusters along the leaves and stalks. What you see in gardens, and what is sold in flower shops, is purple beautyberry, with its clusters of autumn berries.

There is also a variety of Japanese beautyberry called *murasaki modoki* in Japanese, whose purple berries are larger than those of the Japanese beautyberry, and another variety, *shiro shikibu* in Japanese, which has white berries, although in English these are both considered Japanese beautyberry.

Leiden in the Netherlands is famous as the birthplace of the painter Rembrandt. Some years ago I went to arrange flowers there. Among the varieties which our branch members kept bringing for me to arrange were a number that I knew from Japan. Often when I go abroad I find that even in the wholesale flower markets, the assortment of plants is very limited compared to what I find in Japan, but in Leiden I was thrilled to find many different varieties. The climax came when I discovered the Japanese beautyberry among them.

Japanese Beautyberry

Leiden was also the home of Philipp Franz von Siebold (1796-1866). He was German by birth, but came to Japan to serve as a doctor to the Dutch trading post at Dejima in Nagasaki during the Sakoku ("closed country") isolationist period. When he left Japan, he took with him a large number of documents and objects of daily use, including many plant samples and seeds. You can view these at Siebold House and at the Royal Museum of Natural History, while the University of Leiden's botanical gardens have plants grown from the seeds and samples that he carried home. I much regretted that I did not have time to visit.

With this backstory in mind, I realized it was possible that what I held in my hand might have sprouted from one of Siebold's seeds. What generation might it be by now? It was thrilling to think I might be arranging the descendant of a flower that Dr. Siebold had taken from Japan almost two centuries before. I even found myself almost wondering if he had known that I would come and had brought it back for me.

Back in Tokyo, in the autumn, when we were using beautyberry in class, I told this story. One student pointed out that when they arranged beautyberry the berries fell to the ground and a major cleanup was necessary. Another student chimed in and added that it happened even if you gave them plenty of water. Everyone else nodded in agreement.

Beautyberry is one of the ornamental plants that epitomizes autumn. At least once a year I like to use this material, so rare abroad, in our flower arrangements. As I undid the beautyberry's newspaper wrapping, I thought to myself, "Such prettily colored berries, and yet what a nuisance it is!" The berries tumbled out in all directions, and, as I cut the knotted string, more spilled out, just as if they had been waiting all along to show off their purple glossiness. They rolled and scattered, over and under the table.

We all had a good laugh. The plant is exasperating! 🌱

37 Happy Tree

Camptotheca acuminate

旱蓮木 *kanrenboku*

It has been half a century since I had my first lessons in *ikebana*, but even so there are many plants I know nothing about, not only in other parts of the world but even here within Japan. So once when I had work in Osaka, I set out looking forward to discovering plants that grow only in that region, but not in Tokyo where I live.

I called a florist there that was referred by someone who knew my preference in flowers, hoping there might be some materials I could use in my demonstration. The florist recommended the happy tree. Never having heard of it before, I had to ask him how to write the name in Japanese characters.

At the florist's, as I unrolled the rough, paper wrapping it came in, a slender branch with a single fruit hanging from its tip emerged. This was at a time of year when most plants bear only red and yellow fruit or berries, so this fruit, which was a pretty pale green, looked extremely fresh in comparison. Looking closely, I saw clusters of small, green, banana-shaped fruit, which together formed small spheres. At my touch, these "minibananas" dropped off easily. I picked one up, and noticed that it had three definite edges.

Small, slender twigs stemmed from the sides of the larger branches, from the tips of which the globes dangled, making a lovely spectacle, as if green planets, large and small, danced in space. Later, back at my hotel, I cut one of the "bananas" into slices and examined it. The tip of the knife had touched a kind of semisolid core, which may have actually been the seed. Eventually, the fruit would probably turn brown as it matured. I learned subsequently that the happy

Happy Tree

tree, which is so vital and full of life, has pharmaceutical properties and is being studied in medical research.

The happy tree can reach over ten meters (thirty feet) high and has large and glossy green leaves that are distinctly veined. When summer comes, I look forward to seeing its pale green, almost white flowers, which resemble the flowers of the Japanese aralia when seen from a distance. The happy tree is native to southern China. Perhaps with all those seeds encased in the banana-shaped fruit, the "happy tree" was associated with fertility, hence its name. Certainly looking at this tree makes me happy.

We see the round fruit of the happy tree dangling down from its branches late in the fall, about the same time human beings are starting to think about Christmas. The timing makes me think that mother nature is joining in the spirit of the season with her own special ornaments for the coming holidays. 🌱

38 Chinese Quince

Pseudocydonia sinensis

榠樝 *karin*

For most people in Japan, the word *karin*, or Chinese quince, evokes memories of cough drops or cough medicine.

Besides vitamin C, quince contains citric acid and malic acid. Although the fruit is not suited for eating raw, quince can be made into fruit liqueur or candied fruit. The fruit of the ordinary quince (*marumero* in Japanese) is similar in shape and color to that of the Chinese quince, but while it too belongs to the rose family (*rosaceae*), it belongs to the genus Cydonia, while the Chinese quince belongs to the genus Chaenomeles.

The flowers of the Chinese quince, which bloom in spring, are pale red with five petals. It is almost impossible to imagine that in autumn these delicate flowers give way to such large fruit, each weighing a pound or more.

It is quite a spectacle when they ripen. The fruit appears to be attached directly to the branches, which sag and look ready to collapse under the excess weight. So totally out of proportion is the size of the fruit to the girth of the branches that are supposed to support it, the fruit tumbles heavily to the ground, leaving the branches bare.

When we need a branch of Chinese quince with lots of fruit on it for an *ikebana* demonstration, we have to improvise since all we have are the bare branches or those with only one or two of the quince still hanging on. We take the fallen fruit and make a hole in the top of each. After cutting the smaller branches on a diagonal, we stick the fruit onto the branches. Among ourselves we call this *sashimi*, or "pierced fruit." If you take a closer look at the fruit-laden

Chinese Quince

branch, it may appear unnatural, but in light of the weight of the quince and the difficulties there are in transporting branches intact, it cannot be helped.

It is not always possible in *ikebana* to have every composition appear completely natural, as in this case. The role of the *ikebana* artist here is to interpret, and to capture, the beauty of nature for the viewer.

Like the Chinese quince, there are many amazing things in the natural world. Take pollination, for example, which is a joint exercise between plants and animals. To make the seeds for the next generation of plants, it is the birds and insects that do the transporting of the pollen from plant to plant. A cleverly designed structure protects plants from extremes of temperature and helps insure the plant's survival. In Oceania, I have heard, there are plants whose fruit splits open and sends seeds flying far away during the wildfires that occur naturally every year.

Picking up a fallen quince, I thought about its odd behavior for a while. Perhaps there is a straightforward explanation for it: the Chinese quince grows too big to hang on its branch so it falls. Or this: does the quince perhaps "realize" that the girth of the branch from which it hangs can no longer support it and so drops before it gets any bigger? I doubt animals could knock it off. With fruit this size, a bird would have a hard time. Since the fruit in its raw state is inedible for human beings, animals too might find it off-putting, supposing they did manage to climb up and reach one. Another possibility: the Chinese quince, in its wisdom, arranges things so that it grows bigger and bigger and then at the perfect time—speaking, that is, for its descendants, who will grow from its seeds—falls. Behold, I've turned into a philosopher!

When I picked up the egg-shaped fruit, its slightly olive green, yellow exterior felt a little oily. From beneath its gleaming skin floated up a uniquely sweet and pungent fragrance. 🌱

39 Chrysanthemum

Chrysanthemum x moriolium

菊 *kiku*

I was once astonished to see masses of large, plump chrysanthemums in the lobby of a Japanese-run hotel in Vienna. There were flowers of yellow, white, and pink, and some with petals that were yellow on the outside and dark red within. The glass vases that held the flowers echoed the sparkling crystal chandeliers and ornate, gold tables and chairs that embellished the all-white foyer. In amongst them, rare, antique ceramic dolls and stately candle stands stood on display. In a corner of my heart I think of chrysanthemums as uniquely Asian so I was a bit surprised.

Chrysanthemums are believed to be native to China, but they are now found all over the world. In Japan, they are particularly important. Even without referencing Ruth Benedict's *The Chrysanthemum and the Sword*, they have become a symbol of this country, as closely linked to it for the Japanese as is the flowering cherry.

Among the five traditional Japanese festivals (*gosekku*), the last one of the year is the Chrysanthemum Festival, also known as the Double Ninth or Chongyang Festival, which falls on the ninth day of the ninth month in the lunar calendar. Draping chrysanthemums in filmy cotton the night before, our ancestors would begin the festival day with a cleansing of themselves with the dew-impregnated cloth. Then they would drink saké in which chrysanthemum petals floated, which they believed had medicinal powers, and pray for longevity and eternal youth. These days autumn brings exhibitions of single chrysanthemums the size of a human head; painstakingly

Chrysanthemum

grown, beautiful cascade chrysanthemums; and chrysanthemum dolls modelled on figures from history.

Today quantities of chrysanthemums are imported from abroad as well as grown in Japan. Over time our way of looking at this flower has changed as we have seen the many different forms it takes with its many colors. The *chu-giku*, or medium-sized chrysanthemum, yellow or white, and about six centimeters in diameter (two and a half inches), has been used in Buddhist ceremonies since ancient times, but these days we also have the round ping-pong, or pom-pom, mum, which you sometimes see even in bridal bouquets, and the bright green chrysanthemum, which the ancients most likely never saw.

In order to show off the beauty of the line of the stem, the leaves, as well as the small leaves called "leaf buds," are sometimes stripped off, which has the added benefit of releasing the chrysanthemum's natural fragrance. Some people think that chrysanthemums have an aversion to metal, so they use their hands (instead of scissors) to strip off the leaves and break the stem. This is thought to be the secret of the flowers' longevity, but in fact even when the leaves dry up and die, the chrysanthemum's flower itself continues to bloom beautifully. Herein lies the true nature of the chrysanthemum, and we can learn from it.

In Japan the chrysanthemum is a symbol and a stylized design. Each family traditionally has its own family crest, whose design is often based on a plant. Stylized chrysanthemums appear in such crests not only by themselves, but often in combination with other motifs.

The chrysanthemum's varieties seem to increase almost daily, some so unusual that you wonder if they are really chrysanthemums. A few of the many current varieties are: the narrow-petalled *Sagagiku* chrysanthemum, originating in the Saga area of Kyoto; "matchsticks chrysanthemum" or "Korean mum," whose petals look like diagonally cut tubes; the large-flowered "spider mum" with its long, thin petals, which is called *itogiku*, or thread mum, in Japanese; and the "spray mum," developed in Europe from a Japanese variety and then

Chrysanthemum

returned to Japan.

Were I to be asked which variety of chrysanthemum holds the most charm for me, it would be the tiny, native, wild-growing mums with small, white petals that spring up in the countryside, or the ones that are planted along the backstreets and left to grow as they will. As they come into bloom in the fading autumn, their twisted, tangled stems and loam-coated leaves evoke a feeling of the passing of time. Bathed in the generous light of autumn, their life shines. ❦

Winter

WINTER

40 Japanese Snake Gourd

Trichosanthes cucumeroides

烏瓜 *karasuuri*

If you are wandering through a withered field or near some bare-branched trees and come across a vermilion, with a hint of green, egg-shaped fruit hanging from long vines, you have met Japanese snake gourd. Tendrils extend from the vines' nodes and twine around other plants, hanging down in a sort of careless, cheerful way.

"Crow gourd" (*karasu-uri*) is the Japanese name for this plant, and there are a number of theories about its etymology, ranging from one that claims that crows, which are omnivorous, eat it, to one that claims that not even a crow would deign to peck at it. In fact, crows show no interest in it as food. But when I let my imagination go, I can see that against this late autumn scenery, where the temperature has begun to drop, the snake gourd's vermilion shade and the blackness of the crows make a fresh and lovely contrast. This reminds me of yet another theory, which resonates more with me, namely, that the name was originally written not with Chinese characters that mean "crow gourd," but with homophonous ones that mean "Chinese vermilion gourd," because its color resembled the vermilion ink-stick from China.

In summer, the snake gourd blooms for a single night, with white flowers. The blossoms are surprisingly delicate, with lace-like edges. They make their existence known as they swiftly open wide in what almost seems a gesture of invitation to hawkmoths and other nec-tar-sipping moths, blooming with all their might in order to insure they will leave descendants behind. I once had the good fortune to come across the flowers in bloom during a summer night's walk with

Japanese Snake Gourd

Japanese Snake Gourd

some friends. They stood out clearly even in the darkness, but none of us knew that they were the flowers of the Japanese snake gourd until much later. There is quite a distance between the appearance of the gourd when in flower and the gourd with its fruit.

The Japanese snake gourd is a dioecious plant.

There is another variety of the Japanese snake gourd (*kikara-su-uri*), which has yellow fruit. Many adults today in Japan must remember it nostalgically as the main ingredient in what is now called baby powder, for it was used to treat heat rash in children.

Another name for Japanese snake gourd is *tamazusa*, which means "letter" (in the sense of written message), probably because of the folded configuration of its seeds. The life cycle of the Japanese snake gourd unfolds dramatically, beginning with those vivid white flowers, then progressing to the lustrous red fruit, and ending with the somewhat oddly shaped seeds.

The Japanese snake gourd carries a message from nature, reminding us, even as it cheerfully displays its fruit under the clear autumn skies, that the season is reaching its end and soon the real winter will be upon us.

41 Flowering Quince

Chaenomeles speciosa

木瓜 *boke*

In haiku, and elsewhere, some winter season words are made up of the name of a plant that blooms in a different season with the prefix for "cold" or "winter" added to it. In Japanese, these plants include the camellia, the rose, and the quince. With the character for "cold" added to its name, the quince is known as *kan-boke* in Japanese and as "winter flowering quince" or simply "flowering quince" in English. Many plants have berries, but in this season when there are few shrubs, the bright color of the flowering quince lights up our *ikebana* displays and is a prized flower material.

Many years ago Raisa Gorbachev, wife of Soviet leader Mikail Gorbachev, was introduced to *ikebana* during a state visit to Japan. One of our most senior teachers was asked to create an *ikebana* arrangement in front of the guests, showing the process from start to finish. Since the guests were on a very tight schedule, the teacher wanted to focus exclusively on her arrangement and asked me, her junior, to explain as she went along.

In a special room for receiving VIP guests, Mme. Gorbachev watched the demonstration from the comfort of a sofa. The flowering quince which the florist had carefully selected for this important occasion had thick branches and big, scarlet blossoms overflowing with life. When it was brought in, Mme. Gorbachev leaned forward and asked, "What is that flower called?" The interpreter at once told her the name in Russian. As I remember it, I explained that in addition to the scarlet of the flowering quince then being arranged, the plant could also have flowers of pale red, white, and red mixed

Flowering Quince

with white, and in arranging them, you had to be careful of thorns.

After the demonstration was over, the teacher, the interpreter, and I got on the elevator with Mme. Gorbachev and her tall bodyguards in order to bid her farewell. As the door closed, Mme. Gorbachev asked me, "What is the name of that red flower in Japanese?" and I said it slowly, separating the syllables carefully, "*bo-ke.*" Leaning a little against the wall as the elevator descended, Mme. Gorbachev repeated the word to herself, "*bo-ke, bo-ke,*" as though to store it in memory.

As soon as the elevator reached the ground floor and the doors opened, her security people outside instantly encircled the vehicle in which she was to ride, looking around vigilantly. Mme. Gorbachev resumed her public persona and, in the vehicle preceded by police cars and white motorbikes, disappeared down the avenue, which was closed to traffic.

I think it was a few years later that I learned of Mme. Gorbachev's death.

Now, when I sometimes do demonstrations for state guests to Japan and other important people, this is my hope: that the power of our plants can bring some sense of relaxation and joy to their busy lives. With this hope, the memory of Mme. Gorbachev's scarlet, flowering quince always returns. 🌱

42 Mistletoe

Viscum album
宿木 *yadorigi*

When the trees shed their leaves and you can see the sky, look up towards the treetops and you will see thick, round, green masses nestled among the branches. They look like birds' nests but actually are parasitic plants called mistletoe. Mistletoe has many varieties, but the one found in Japan since ancient times has thick leaves. When the berries are ripe, they are pale yellow.

In Japan, mistletoe attaches itself to large trees like cherry, beech, zelkova, hackberry, and oak, and extracts nutrients from the tree to which it is attached, while at the same time its leaves carry out photosynthesis. The many fluffy, round shapes sprinkled like dark green froth among the trees almost seem to create an artificial landscape.

The first time I saw mistletoe was not in a natural setting but in a city, in the Roppongi district of Tokyo. It must have been almost forty years ago. Foreigners were beginning to appear in rather large numbers in Roppongi, and, above the entrance to a large flower shop, I noticed some holly and mistletoe tied together with a red ribbon. I had no idea what it might mean.

At Christmas, in America and in Europe, they often hang European mistletoe with white berries over a doorway or at the entrance to a room. This custom may have originated in Celtic and Scandinavian myths and in the traditions of certain parts of Europe.

These days, even in Japan you often see mistletoe in the large flower shops of major cities at Christmas time. But deprived of their host trees, the plants become quite brittle and dry, and the green, branched stalks tend to break off. If you absentmindedly crush a

Mistletoe

berry from a broken branch, a viscous liquid will seep out and stick to your fingers, so care is necessary in handling it. You can see a well-protected seed inside the translucent membrane of the berry. In Japan this membrane is a greenish, pale yellow, but I am told that in Europe it is white.

Carried by the birds, mistletoe's sticky berries sprout and firmly lay down their roots on tree branches. This plant's strong life force explains why it appears in myths to possess spiritual powers. Mistletoe is also believed to bring good luck and happiness to lovers. It delivers a host of good things.

Until not too long ago, there was a tacit understanding in some Christmas traditions that it was permissible to kiss any girl or woman standing beneath the mistletoe. This is the background to the popular song "I Saw Mommy Kissing Santa Claus," with the line "Underneath the mistletoe last night." Many singers have recorded this song, including Michael Jackson, who sang it as a cute little kid in a high key when he was in the Jackson Five, the group he had with his older brothers. But if Michael Jackson as a child is too far back for you, then there is Mariah Carey singing, "I'm just gonna keep on waiting/Underneath the mistletoe," in "All I Want for Christmas is You."

For a plant that never touches the earth, mistletoe seems to be quite busy in arranging romantic trysts between all sorts of people in all sorts of places, almost as if it were gaily throwing the kisses itself.

Mistletoe

43 The Igiri Tree

Idesia polycarpa
飯桐 *iigiri*

The berries of the igiri tree hang down in bright scarlet clusters that make an eye-catching sight in late autumn. The Japanese name is *iigiri* and is written with the characters for "rice" and "empress tree," perhaps because in olden times people used to wrap rice in its large leaves or use the leaves as platters for serving rice.

There is another name for this plant as well, *nantengiri*, which must have been inspired by its lustrous round berries, for in color and shape they resemble the berries of the *nanten*, or nandina. In its berry season, the igiri tree can grow up to fifteen meters (fifty feet) high and stands out dramatically, not only to human beings but to birds as well. Just as you are thinking of enjoying a distant view of the berries, you realize—the berries are gone! As a florist who specializes in plants for *ikebana* once told me, "If you want to use them as materials for your *ikebana*, when they are at their prettiest, you need to protect them from the birds with nets as high up as possible."

I once saw an igiri tree as summer neared its end. The berries were green, and you would never have imagined their late autumn splendor; yet, still unripe, they seemed slight, even delicate, and had their own attraction. I have heard that there are also igiri trees with white berries rather than red ones but have not seen them myself.

As autumn deepens, the berries form clusters that can reach twenty centimeters (eight inches) in length, and they retain their red color on the branches even when the large leaves fall. At this point, you can cut them off the branches with no fear of the berries suddenly falling off or their skin shriveling, even if they are not put

The Igiri Tree

in water for some time. This must be one of the reasons that you often see the berries of the igiri tree used as materials in exhibitions held at this season.

The bark of the igiri tree certainly does resemble that of the empress tree. They say that the wood of the empress tree is used to make *tansu* chests and wooden sandals called *geta* because its wood is light in comparison to that of other trees. Pick up a branch of the igiri tree, even one laden with berries, and you will find it lighter than it looks.

Almost as if the plant had inherent wisdom which directed it to expose as much of itself to the sun as possible, its horizontal branches fan out like spreading wings, and the berry clusters are so positioned that they do not overlap or get entangled with one another.

If you are fortunate enough to catch sight of the berries of the igiri tree at this season, be sure to pay close attention to their shape and color. Try looking up a little on your daily walk to see if there are any there, for even in the center of a city you may discover an igiri tree with its spectacular berries closer than you think. Providing, that is, that you get there before the birds… 🌾

The Igiri Tree

44 Poinsettia

Euhorbia pulcherrima
ポインセチア *poinsechia*

When I went to Mexico, I was amazed to see poinsettias as high as five-meter (sixteen-foot) trees proudly blooming. In Japan, the only time we see these flowers, with the exceptions of the southern parts such as Okinawa or Ogasawara, is during the Christmas season, and mostly grown in pots.

What seems to be this plant's blossoms are actually bract leaves, and they come in various colors—red, cream, pink, dappled, and gradated. There is a great variety in size and shape among imported cut flowers, including ones with undulating bract leaves.

If you cut a stalk off from a potted plant, you will notice a white liquid ooze out. This troublesome substance makes it difficult for water to be drawn up into the stalk. One of the ways to enjoy this plant for a long time is to cut it to whatever length you wish, wrap it in damp newspaper one to one and one-half inches above the cut, then burn the cut end until it carbonizes, and place it in water at once. Once it sizzles, you're done. You can put it into a container without cutting any more off, and it will take up water.

The poinsettia is native to Mexico. The Japanese name, *shojoboku* (literally "*shojo* tree") comes from the *shojo,* which is a mythical creature with a red face and flaming red hair. The *shojo* is said to be a large ape fond of alcohol. I would like to use this plant in our flower arrangements not only at Christmas but at other times as well. Why should we use it only for the one short season? I wish Christmas were a little earlier too so I could enjoy this plant a little longer, but perhaps that is just another instance of the tail wagging the dog, the rescheduling of a holiday for our personal convenience.

As soon as December 25 has come and gone, everyone starts rushing to get ready for the New Year celebrations, and the poinsettia disappears from flower-shop prominence. It's a little sad to see them languishing in the back. It makes me feel that something is pushing me towards the year's end, even though I'd like to enjoy the Christmas spirit a little longer. 🌱

Poinsettia

45 Heavenly Bamboo

Nandina domestica

南天 *nanten*

I first met heavenly bamboo when I was quite small. Someone gave me a box of celebratory rice with red beans *(sekihan),* and when I opened it I saw, in addition to sesame salt, which I was used to, flat leaves on a stem, which seemed very strange.

In Japanese, this plant is called *nanten.* I was told later on that its leaves are used at times of celebration because *nan* is homonymous with the character *nan* which means misfortune, and *ten* is homonymous with *ten,* the stem of the verb *tenjiru,* which means to change, so *nanten* is a pun on "change misfortune"—meaning good luck.

Which reminds me—a tree planted in a corner of our garden when I was growing up was definitely heavenly bamboo. I later learned that it stood in the "demons' gate" corner of the garden, which was thought to face an unlucky direction, and realized that it must have been planted there to ward off evil. Heavenly bamboo leaves are also thought to have the power to detoxify poisons, and that is supposed to be another reason for placing them on top of red bean rice.

Heavenly bamboo owes its frequent presence in gardens to the pleasure it offers from season to season. In some varieties, the innocent, fresh green of the new buds turns to masses of white flowers from late spring to early summer, and then from autumn through winter we have the bright red of the berries and the wide-spreading, vibrantly colored leaves to enjoy.

The branches are surprisingly hard, as you will discover when you try to cut them with *ikebana* scissors. The inner part of the bark is yellowish where the cut has been made.

Heavenly Bamboo

The berries are not exclusively red; some are also white. When arranging the berries of heavenly bamboo in *ikebana*, a bit of care is sometimes necessary, because even when the glossy berries ripen and turn red, the branches remain quite firm and do not bend as much as with other plants. If you are careless and do not allow for this, the balance of the arrangement will suffer, and, far from avoiding bad luck, you will find that the water-filled container, or *kenzan* needle-point holder, can tip over. A mad rush to avoid disaster will follow.

I have recently learned of a new *ikebana* "trick" from florists, in which they puncture a hole in a branch of heavenly bamboo that has lost its berries, and then re-attach berries to the branch to make it look more natural.

It may be worth mentioning that the species (also the genus) name "nandina" comes from *nanten*, the Japanese name for heavenly bamboo. Heavenly bamboo, like Chinese quince, is a source of cough medicine. You often see candy and cough drops made from it.

Many years have passed and the riddle of that leaf that so puzzled me as a child is now solved. Together with a fond childhood memory of using its red berries for the eyes of the snow rabbits we made when the snow fell, I think from now on I will be looking at the heavenly bamboo and its berries with a new kind of interest. 🌿

46 Tsukubane

Buckleya lanceolata

衝羽根 *tsukubane*

"I hesitated to show it to an *ikebana* teacher, but I'm coming to see you with a *tsukubane* plant," said a friend of mine, to which I replied, feigning knowledge that I did not have, "Do you mean a glossy abelia, *tsukubane utsugi*? I know what that is." As soon as I had a chance, I looked up *tsukubane* in my botanical dictionary, and sure enough there it was, though I'd never heard of it before.

How grateful I was when my friend arrived by taxi with a single branch carefully packed in a cardboard box. "It's really cute," she said. It is one of those plants that you must place a special order for from a flower shop, for it is not commonly sold. When my friend explained that it was used as an ornament during the formal tea ceremony and at New Year's, it made perfect sense.

Four bracts enclose the fruit, exactly like the feathers on a shuttlecock, which is called *hane* in Japanese. When you cut off the leaves around it, the shuttlecock shape becomes even more pronounced. I rushed to take a photo, but the leaves had dried out and already wrinkled so they fell off with a rustle as soon as they were touched. This had the effect, however, of making the fruit even more visible.

According to the botanical dictionary, this plant, which belongs to the *Santalaceae* family, is native to Japan. Were this not the case, it is unlikely that its name would be *tsukubane*, which refers to the shuttlecock used in the traditional Japanese game *hanetsuki*, which is played at New Year's and resembles badminton. Reminiscing on the old days when I was a little girl, I remember how I cherished playing the game in my colorful New Year's kimono and how I would fold its long sleeves under my arms. These days it is rare to see children playing *hanetsuki*.

I also learned that the fruit can be roasted or pickled. Come to think of it, I remember once having it served to me at a rather upscale Japanese restaurant somewhere. But I don't recall the experience inspiring me to try using it in *ikebana*.

When the fruits ripen, they use the bracts as wings and fly far away, carried by the wind. How well this lovely and charming *ikebana* material lives up to its name, flying through the air just like a shuttlecock. 🦋

Tsukubane

47 Glabrous Sarcandra

Sarcandra glabra (Thunb.) Nakai

千両 *senryou*

During the hustle and bustle of December, the wholesale flower market has a special, once-a-year auction for pine in all its varieties, followed then by another auction, a week or so later, for glabrous sarcandra. Only florists with special admission permits are allowed to bid.

Glabrous sarcandra is divided into different groupings according to its leaves and berries, color, overall length, and so on, each priced accordingly when sold in flower shops. After purchasing it, florists beat and crush the stem bottom and place it in water. After some time, they change the water, wrap the plant in paper, and put it away. Just as Christmas trees and poinsettias disappear, pine and glabrous sarcandra replace them in the flower shops.

Glabrous sarcandra belongs to the sarcandra family. Its jagged, glossy green leaves contrast vividly with its crimson-orange berries, and, when added to New Year's flower arrangements, it contributes to the festive mood of the season. There is also the *Sarcandra glaber* var. *flava*, a plant which has no English name; it has yellow berries.

When cut, glabrous sarcandra must absorb water to prevent the fruit from withering and the leaves from drooping. To insure that, we remove the excess leaves, as well as those that are damaged or otherwise imperfect, and then pound the stem bottom again. But you must be careful. Once the stem takes up a good quantity of water and the berries ripen, they can easily fall off if over-watered.

In contrast to glabrous sarcandra, whose berries sit atop the leaves, the red berries of the coral bush (also called coralberry tree)

Glabrous Sarcandra

hang down below the leaves on straight stems. Some coral bushes have white berries. In Japanese, glabrous sarcandra is written with characters that mean "one thousand gold pieces," or *ryo*, a monetary unit, while the characters for the coral bush are "ten thousand gold pieces," or *ryo*. There is a fanciful folk etymology that says the berries of the coral bush hang lower down than those of the glabrous sarcandra because "ten thousand *ryo*" is the heavier of the two.

In addition to these two plants whose names are written with characters that relate to money, there is the "one hundred *ryo*" plant, or Ardisia crispa. The Ardisia japonica is written with characters that mean "ten *ryo*." All belong to the Myrsinaceae family. Of course there is also a "one *ryo*" plant, which belongs to the Rubiaceae family. Its botanical name is *damnacanthus indicus*, but it has no English name, and in Japanese it is commonly called *aridoshi*, literally, "where ants pass," so called, it is said, because it is so thorny that only ants can make their way through it.

In parts of western Japan, *damnacanthus indicus* is included in flower arrangements at New Year's because it is thought to augur lifelong prosperity. The characters of its name, "ant-passing" are a near-homonym for the phrase *issho ari doshi,* which means "having it [money] all your life." This is really carrying punning and magical thinking to extremes, it seems to me.

I heard that a glabrous sarcandra seedling that sprouted berries appeared in the garden of one of my students, perhaps dropped there by a bird. This inspires feelings of gratitude in me, a promise of good things for the coming year.

An ordinary person, not motivated by money, I am more than satisfied with making *ikebana* arrangements out of the glabrous sarcandra with its abundant clusters of red berries shining against those lush green leaves. That is reward enough for me. 🌱

48 Pine

Pinus
松 *matsu*

In early December when we order plants for the last class of the year, which is always devoted to arrangements for the New Year, I ask each of my students, "What kind of pine do you want to use for your arrangement?"

Because there are so many varieties, each with its own unique character, it is difficult to know which type to choose. There is the slim, straight *wakamatsu* young pine; the uprooted *nebikimatsu* pine with its interesting short foliage, which is often sold with its roots intact; the yellow-speckled dragon-eye *janome-matsu* pine; the *goyo matsu* Japanese white pine on which more than five small, dark green leaves sprout from a cluster; and the *daiosho* longleaf pine with elongated leaves that can be over thirty centimeters (twelve inches) long.

When the time comes to make a decision so that we can place our order, the students converse among themselves and share their thoughts. One says, "Last year I did an arrangement using young pine, so this year I'm going to do one with uprooted pine," while another remarks, "This year was the Year of the Snake so I used snake-eye [dragon-eye] pine but maybe I'll arrange a different kind of pine for the coming year."

On the one day of the year when we use pine, the class bubbles with excitement. Words of advice fly around the room freely. "A new year is beginning so be especially careful to arrange the pine as attractively as possible." "Please remove any bent or browned leaves before you begin." "If you're using a *kenzan* needle-point holder, please be sure your heavy pine bough is standing up straight and held securely."

Those who do not bring leather or cotton working gloves will find their hands covered in pine resin, so they are offered hand cream to take it off. They spread the cream on their hands, use a tissue to wipe it off, and then wash with soap and hot water.

By the way, have you ever wondered why we always use pine for New Year's decorations? In Japan, evergreen trees stand out prominently among the leafless, deciduous trees of late winter. The pine is special to us at this season. With its unchanging green, it is considered a *yorishiro*, a temporary abode, for the benevolent *kami* (gods) of the New Year. The custom is to place an ornamental pine arrangement on both sides of your front gate.

At the wholesale flower market, there is one day at the very beginning of December when the pines arrive all at once, and the pine market begins. Pine boughs that are sold at auction that day will not appear in retail shops until after Christmas when the florists deem the time is ripe, close to the start of the New Year's holiday. It is a good idea to buy them as soon as they appear in flower shops in order to have the best selection.

When the year-end lessons finish, I give each student especially long *mizuhiki* decorative cords, longer than those usually used, for their pine arrangements. They are 180 centimeters (six-feet) long and either red and white or silver and gold. *Mizuhiki* paper cords are used as decorations for the presentation bags and envelopes we use for gifts and money. On celebratory occasions, they may be red and white or silver and gold, while on unhappy ones (misfortune, death, disaster) they are black and white or else yellow and white. If the event is one that we wish to be a one-time occurrence, such as a wedding or a death, the cords are knotted in such a way that they cannot be undone. If the event is one we hope will recur, such as a birth, exhibition opening, or other celebration, then it is tied so that it can be easily undone.

Many of my students work during the day. Despite their fatigue as they hurry to wrap up the year at their jobs, they come to class in the evening and cheerfully complete their arrangements. Imagine the joy and gratification they experience when, at the end of the class, they see their pine boughs festooned with festive cords that herald the promise of a bright, new year. Their faces glow with pleasure and satisfaction, and I pray for their happiness and well-being in the coming year. 🌱

Pine

KOKA – 166

Afterword

Japanese *ikebana* is said to be the embodiment of the culture of *wa*. The word can be translated as "of or relating to Japan" (as in the expression *washoku*, traditional Japanese food; or *wafuku*, traditional Japanese dress) and "harmony," but more importantly is used to express the essence of the Japanese spirit. *Wa* includes a panoply of human emotions—a sense of concord and empathy as a basis for harmony. I owe this understanding to Kai Hasegawa, whose *The Idea of Wa* was mentioned in the preface to this book.

In *ikebana*, the arranger chooses elements of plants—flowers, leaves, and branches—which have been grown and gathered in a variety of locations, placing them in carefully selected containers which complement their form. While respecting the individuality of the plant materials, the practitioner cuts and bends them as necessary to achieve the right effect. She does not merely impose her own idea or image on the flower material. Rather, she interacts with its distinctive characteristics, so much so that her form of artistry is molded by it. This artistry is not unique to any people but is born from an instinctive interaction with the plant. This is *wa*.

Creating a book resembles the same process.

Janine Beichman agreed to do the translation. Those who know her well will understand how fortunate I was. I cannot find enough words of thanks.

This is the first book I have published in English since the little book *Behind Flowers* in my twenties. My *ikebana* student and former classmate Hiroko Lockheimer, who now lives in California, stepped in on short notice and recruited several experts to help, as well as contributing her own editorial expertise.

I would also like to thank Anne Papantonio for the constant editorial help and support she gave me from New York. She was a longtime resident in Japan, and her knowledge of Japanese culture and her editing skills have helped make this book what it is.

Gary Rust of rustmedia generously contributed his expertise in marketing and broad experience in publishing. Kyoko Ito designed the book and fine-tuned the revisions. I am grateful to both of them.

Ikuyo Munakata Morrison of London, specialist in botany and first director of the London branch of the Sogetsu School, oversaw the botanical and English names of all the plants. Many professional photographers very kindly gave permission for use of their photographs in the book, and friends of professional caliber in photography both in Japan and abroad contributed photographs. The near-instant communication that is now the norm for our age made this book possible, but the most important factor was the devoted support of all of these people. With everyone coming together to respond to all the different issues that arose as the book evolved, I feel that the spirit of *wa* lives in this book.

I have been fortunate to be asked to give demonstrations and teach *ikebana* in many parts of the world by the Sogetsu School of Ikebana, Ikebana International, the Japan Foundation, and others, thanks to the kindness of the *iemoto* (heads) of the Sogetsu School: Sofu Teshigahara, founder of the Sogetsu School; the second *iemoto*, Kasumi Teshigahara; the third, Hiroshi Teshigahara; and the fourth, Akane Teshigahara.

Saki Fukase, widow of the poet and critic Makoto Ooka, kindly gave her permission to use her husband's poem "Flower 1" as the epigraph to the book.

I offer my deepest thanks to all who helped bring this project to fruition.

Koka Fukushima
May 2021

KOKA – 169

Photographs and Illustrations

Photographs

Cover—Yoshiki Nakano
Frontispiece—Yoshiki Nakano
Preface—Yoshiki Nakano

Spring

Summer

Koka Fukushima

About the Author and the Translator

Koka Fukushima, *author*

Born in Tokyo, Koka Fukushima began her study of Sogetsu *ikebana* in 1960. She was fortunate to participate in workshop-lessons given by Sofu Teshigahara, founder of the Sogetsu School of Ikebana, and has studied, or worked, with all subsequent *iemoto* (heads) of the school: Kasumi Teshigahara, Hiroshi Teshigahara, and the present *iemoto*, Akane Teshigahara, in addition to her own teacher, Shinko Yamazaki.

Unofficial ambassador of Japanese culture, she has been giving *ikebana* demonstrations and workshops under the sponsorship of the Sogetsu School, the Japan Foundation, Ikebana International, and the Japanese Ministry of Foreign Affairs, for forty years in almost eighty cities and in over forty countries. She was awarded the FY2013 Foreign Minister's Commendation for her contributions to the promotion of friendship between Japan and other countries.

She holds the distinguished title of Master Instructor of the Sogetsu Headquarters and is a member of the Ikebana International Tokyo founding chapter. While widely known and respected as an *ikebana* artist, she has also gained recognition for her work as a designer of *ikebana* containers in stainless steel and titanium.

Janine Beichman, *translator*

Janine Beichman, Professor Emerita of Daito Bunka University, received the 2019-2020 Japan-United States Friendship Commission Prize for the Translation of Japanese Literature for *Beneath the Sleepless Tossing of the Planets: Selected Poems of Makoto Ooka*.

"**Koka Fukushima brings her lifelong love of flowers to readers** around the world in these forty-eight tales. Her deep sense of love for plants animates her words and conveys to the reader the luminosity and richness of her *ikebana*."
—**Akane Teshigahara**, *Iemoto, Sogetsu School of Ikebana, Tokyo*

"**Koka-sensei's generosity in sharing what she knows is unlimited.** Anyone who reads this book will have a new and wonderful feeling for the forty-eight flowers that are the subjects of these tales."
—**Norman H. Tolman**, *The Tolman Collection, Tokyo*

"**Even before opening your elegant book, I knew that I was in for a** treat and it certainly lived up to expectations."
—**Marion Maule**, *International lecturer and ardent admirer and promoter of Japanese culture, London*

CPSIA information can be obtained
at www.ICGtesting.com
Printed in the USA
LVHW070342101121
702934LV00007B/131/J